PizzA, PickLes, AND APPLe Pie

written and illustrated
by David Rickert

KANE PRESS

AN IMPRINT OF ASTRA BOOKS FOR YOUNG READERS

New York

To Jack and Lily, my two wonderful children

For information about permission to reproduce selections from this book, please contact
permissions@astrapublishinghouse.com.

Kane Press
An imprint of Astra Books for Young Readers, a division of Astra Publishing House
astrapublishinghouse.com
Printed in China

ISBN: 978-1-6626-7013-8 (hc)
ISBN: 978-1-6626-7014-5 (eBook)
Library of Congress Control Number: 2022060879

Library of Congress Cataloging-in-Publication Data
Names: Rickert, David, author.
Title: Pizza, pickles, and apple pie : the stories behind the foods we love
/ written and illustrated by David Rickert.
Description: First edition. | New York : Kane Press, an imprint of Astra
Books for Young Readers, [2023] | Includes bibliographical references
and index. | Summary: Comic-format stories explore the origins and histories of popular
American foods from pizza to apple pie, with activities guiding readers in creating their own
food history stories and art-- Provided by publisher.
Identifiers: LCCN 2022060879 (print) | LCCN 2022060880 (ebook) | ISBN
9781662670138 (hardcover) | ISBN 9781662670145 (ebk)
Subjects: LCSH: Food--History--Juvenile literature. | Food habits--United
States--History--Juvenile literature.
Classification: LCC TX353 .R523 2023 (print) | LCC TX353 (ebook) | DDC
641.3--dc23/eng/20230104
LC record available at https://lccn.loc.gov/2022060879
LC ebook record available at https://lccn.loc.gov/2022060880

First edition

10 9 8 7 6 5 4 3 2 1

Designed by David Rickert.
The text is set in Gill Sans SemiBold.
The speech bubbles are set in Romper DB.
The titles are hand lettered by David Rickert.
The illustrations for this book were created using Procreate on an iPad with finishing touches and
cleanup done in Adobe Photoshop on a MacBook Pro.

Contents

Who Doesn't Love Food?

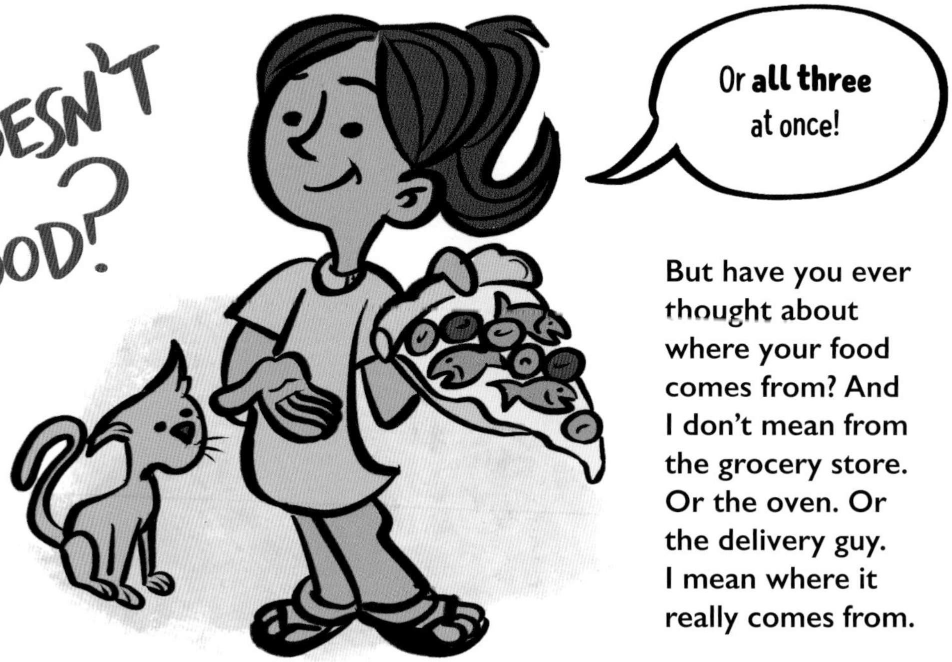
Or **all three** at once!

We all have favorite foods. Yours might be pizza. Or cereal. Or sardines!

But have you ever thought about where your food comes from? And I don't mean from the grocery store. Or the oven. Or the delivery guy. I mean where it really comes from.

For instance, how old do you think your favorite food is? Not how long it's been in the back of the fridge, but when did people start eating it?

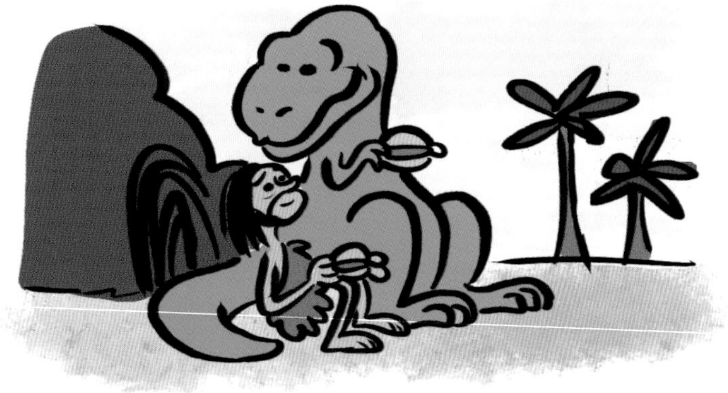

Is your favorite food from another country? If so, how did it get here? By boat? Over land? Through the mail?

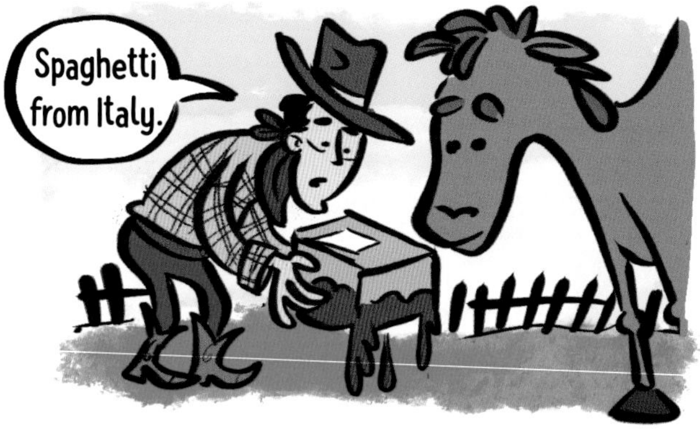
Spaghetti from Italy.

And why did people start eating it? Was it tasty? Was it a convenient snack while working?

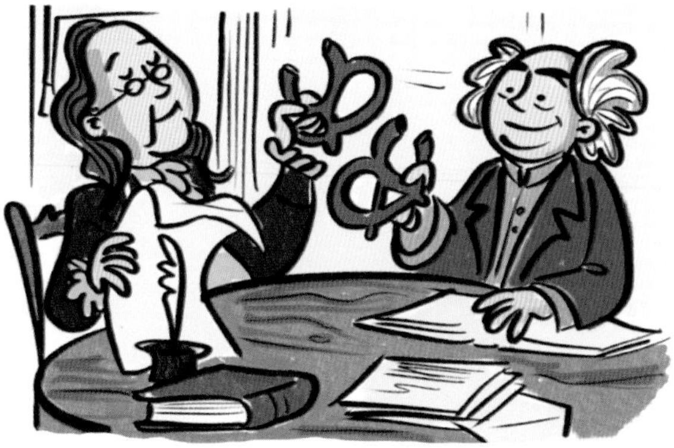

You're going to learn some stories about food that will blow your mind! But first, some basic food facts.

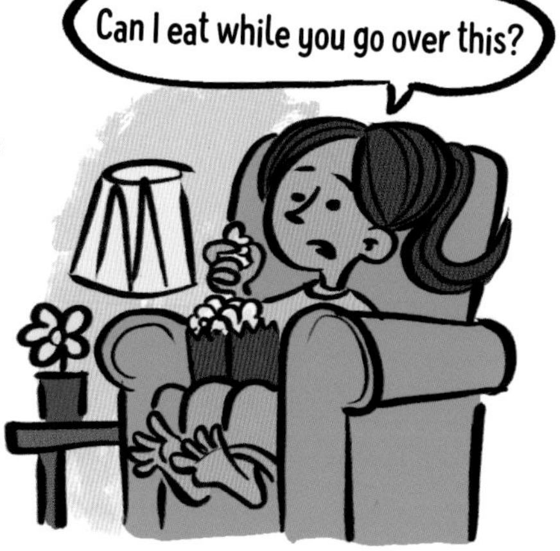
Can I eat while you go over this?

For centuries, people only ate what grew where they lived. If someone wanted food from some other part of the globe—if they even knew it existed—they were out of luck.

Also, for many years, food took work to prepare. People had to make everything they ate from scratch. Some foods could take hours! They didn't have electric stoves or mixers to make it easy, either.

So let's go on a journey. We'll look at some foods we love and the stories of how they came to be. But first, why not grab something to eat before you turn the page?

We'll start at the beginning of the day with

BREAKFAST!

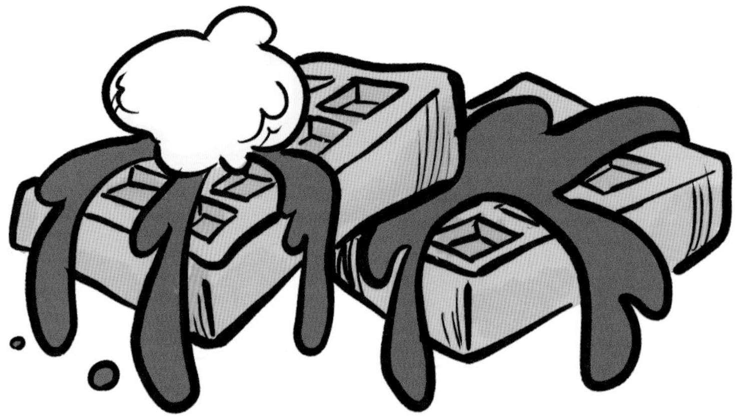

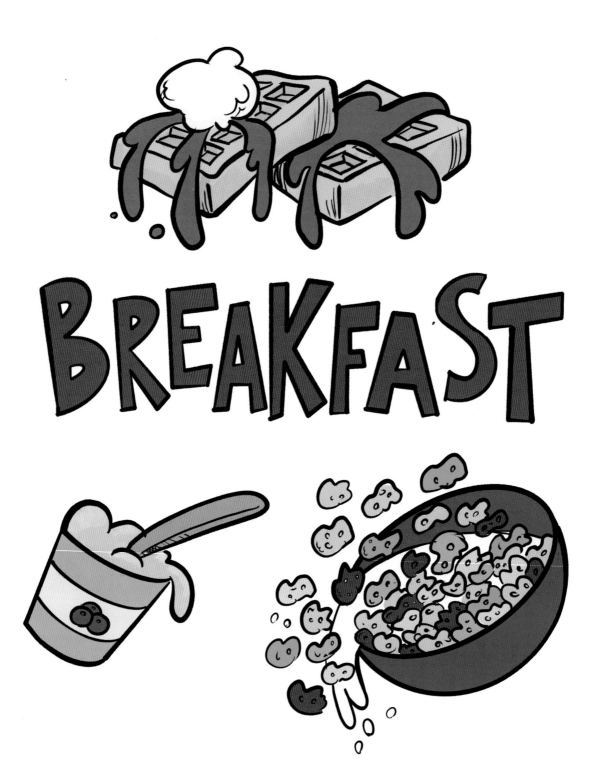

BREAKFAST

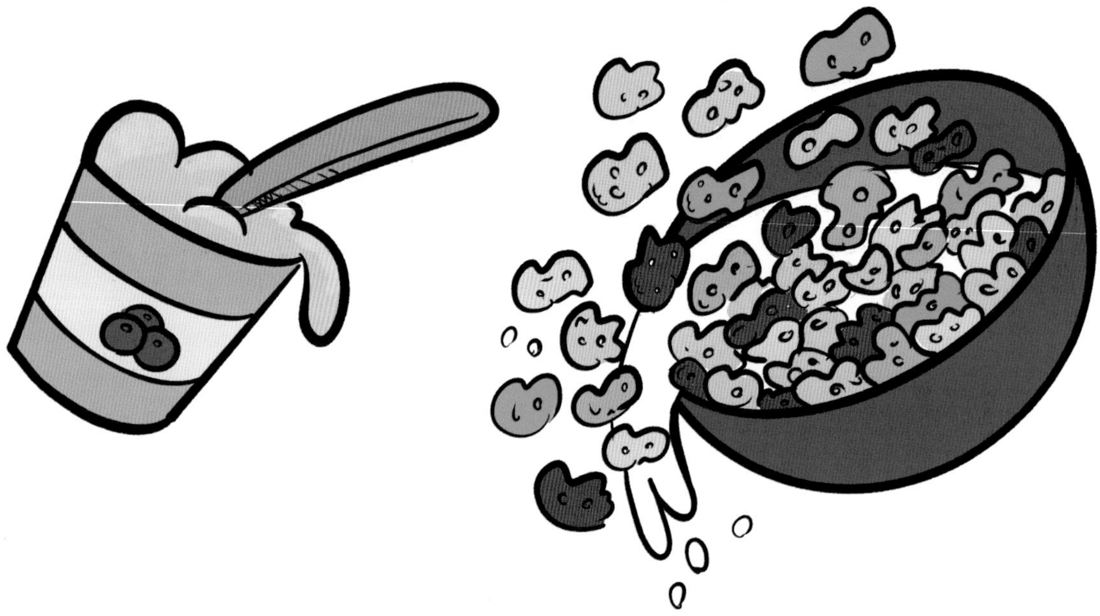

The Sad, Boring World Before Breakfast

Unless you're reading this book at the crack of dawn, you've probably eaten breakfast already. Maybe you poured yourself a bowl of cereal or scarfed down some scrambled eggs.

You might be surprised to know that for centuries, nobody ate breakfast—not as we think of it.

I'm having leftover mashed potatoes!

We have olives, nuts, salad, raisins, or cheese!

And wash it down with wine.

In medieval times in Europe, physicians warned that eating breakfast was dangerous. They believed it caused digestive problems to mix food you just ate with the food you hadn't pooped out yet (don't worry—this isn't true).

Hold on! Have you pooped this morning?

People who worked hard all day did need a morning meal to keep them going. Even then, this might be just a hunk of bread and cheese, and not *our* typical breakfast foods.

So WHAT HAPPENED?

How did we start eating certain foods for breakfast? We'll start with the history behind what 90 percent of kids eat to start their day.

BREAKFAST CEREAL!

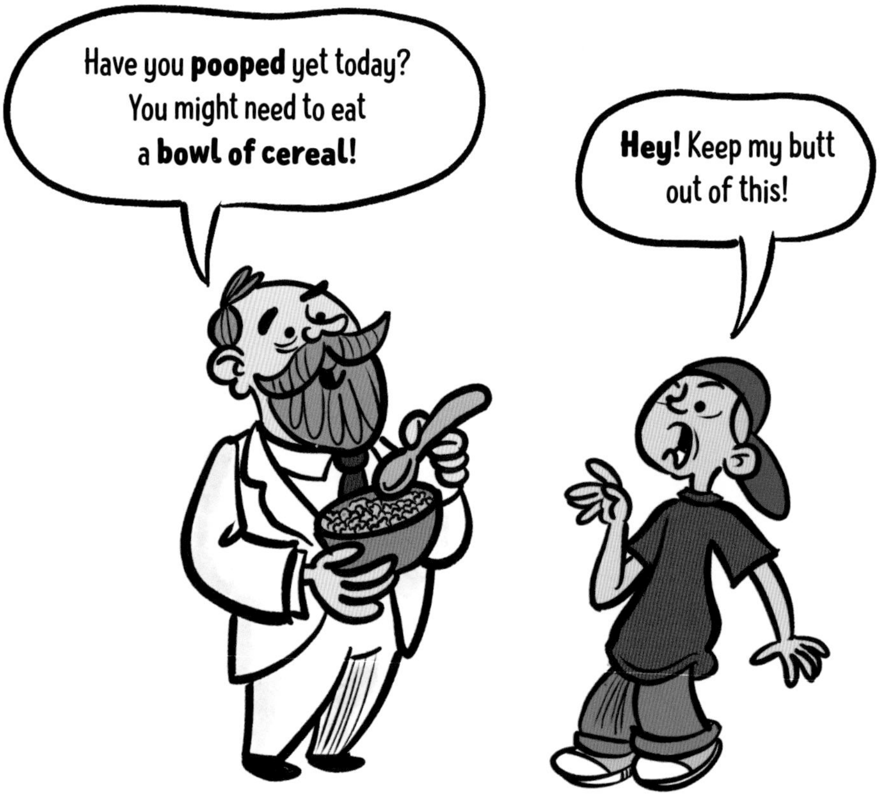
Have you **pooped** yet today? You might need to eat a **bowl of cereal**!
Hey! Keep my butt out of this!

People ate grains all over the world to start their day for centuries. But they didn't come in boxes and weren't shaped into flakes or fun shapes. No marshmallows, either.

Grains became a large part of people's diet because of the rise of agriculture, which allowed people to eat what they could grow rather than what they could gather. A steady food source was now nearby.

For example, Iroquois hunters started their day by eating grains to sustain them throughout the day.

However, in Europe people did enjoy large breakfasts with meat and baked goods. Ham, pies, biscuits—all could be found on the breakfast table.

I beseech you, **bring more food!**

Breakfasts grew larger. And British colonists brought these mighty breakfasts with them to the New World.

America gets a BREAKFAST BELLYACHE

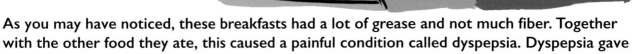

By the middle of the 18th century, a typical American breakfast included mutton chops, bacon, eggs, cornbread, and pie. And maybe some leftovers from the night before. All at one meal!

As you may have noticed, these breakfasts had a lot of grease and not much fiber. Together with the other food they ate, this caused a painful condition called dyspepsia. Dyspepsia gave people a constant bellyache.

Must be all that milking I did today!

Americans wondered what was going on. They thought they were eating good food! Dyspepsia forced people to rethink what they ate.

What you eat is way more important than how much you eat.

Health experts decided that people needed a place where they could take some time off and fix their diet. They opened sanitoriums and fed people a more balanced diet that included a plant-based breakfast.

THE CEREAL SUPERHERO
JOHN HARVEY KELLOGG

*Everyone should be a vegetarian and eat **bland food!** **No spices!***

*And no **dancing** either!*

had a pet cockatoo

Always wore white (easier to see dirt)

believed nuts would be the main food supply in the future

liked enemas (cleaning your bowels with water)

Kellogg was a health fanatic on a mission to cure people's bad diets.

Kellogg was the medical director of a sanitorium in Battle Creek, Michigan. He studied his patients' bowel movements. He believed people should poop 3–4 times daily for optimal health, and thought a good breakfast was the solution.

A good working colon is important! More important than math, even!

*But what can I do to make people eat **healthier?***

Kellogg tirelessly applied science and nutrition to his search for the perfect breakfast food, something easy.

I must find the perfect breakfast!

One day in 1894 . . .

Hmm . . . I left this dough out! It's hard and stale!

Well, I'm not going to let it go to waste.

What happened next was a true cereal miracle! The dough crumbled into flakes. The cornflake was born.

It was a true flake fluke!

I've done it! The perfect breakfast food!

People (and their bowels) will **thank me!**

Kellogg set up a factory in Battle Creek, Michigan, and began to manufacture cornflakes.

I hope they improve the **sewer system . . .**

Battle Creek became the center of the cereal universe. Cereal manufacturers raced to the city to cash in on the cereal craze. By 1902 there were fifty cereal manufacturers in or near Battle Creek.

America developed cereal mania! People could choose from many cereals. Adults loved the healthy, convenient breakfast—all they had to do was pour out cereal and add milk.

Cereal also became a much more popular breakfast for kids. How did that happen?

a spoonful (or more) of sugar!

Cereal companies started adding sugar to cereal to make it taste better. And not just a little bit. A lot. This made it less healthy, but the companies sold more because kids loved the taste. And the more sugar they added, the more cereal they sold.

More.

More!

That's it!

By the end of the 1940s, breakfast cereal contained so much sugar that Kellogg wouldn't have called it cereal.

Companies also spent lots of time and money designing the perfect package and advertising to catch the eyes of children.

Here are some things that worked:

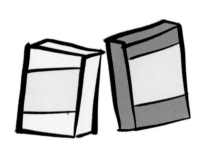

BRIGHT COLORS

CARTOON MASCOTS

ADS ON KIDS' TELEVISION PROGRAMS

And it didn't stop there. Cereal companies kept finding more ways to attract kids' attention.

CHeAP ToYS iN CARdBOARd BoXeS

Another way to attract kids to cereal was prizes. At first, they were part of the box, like a cutout mask, or a cardboard record kids could play on a record player.

But then cereal makers started putting prizes right in the cereal boxes. Companies sought out the best toys to give them the edge over the other cereals.

I don't care what the cereal tastes like. I just want **the toy!**

Eventually plastic molds made toys cheap to produce. And **boy**, were there **great prizes!**

TERRARIUMS

MONSTER FINGER PUPPETS

NAVY FROGMEN

GLOW IN THE DARK PENS

WATCHES

SPY KITS

PINBALL GAMES

9

Bad, Bad Breakfast Cereal

So why are there no prizes in cereal today? In 1972 the Consumer Product Safety Act banned most toy prizes for safety reasons.

They have parts that could **break off** and accidentally be swallowed by **young kids**.

Boo!

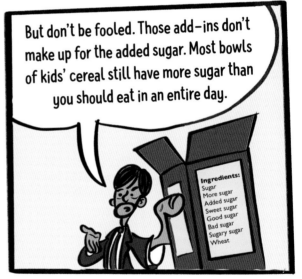

Because of the concerns of parents and children's health experts, manufacturers added essential **vitamins and minerals** to cereals.

IRON RIBOFLAVIN WHOLE GRAINS

DOCTOR

But don't be fooled. Those add-ins don't make up for the added sugar. Most bowls of kids' cereal still have more sugar than you should eat in an entire day.

Ingredients:
Sugar
More sugar
Added sugar
Sweet sugar
Good sugar
Bad sugar
Sugary sugar
Wheat

However, you can find plenty of tasty and healthy cereal options. Healthy cereals are made from whole grains with at least 5 grams of **fiber**, and less than 5 grams of **added** sugar.

And there's another breakfast option that people have known about for years. Centuries, even! And it all began with some herdsmen who let milk sit out for too long.

OLD MILK BECOMES FRESH FOOD

It would be hard to find healthier food than yogurt. And the best thing about it? People have been making it the same way for thousands of years! You can't improve on the method if you try.

In the Neolithic era in what is now Turkey, people raised animals for milk. But not just cows. Camels, sheep, goats, and horses— if it produced milk, they milked it. They knew that any animal's milk was a great food source.

SQUIRT

SQUIRT

SQUIRT

SQUIRT

SQUIRT

Don't even try!

Around the 6th century BCE, Central Asian herdsmen traveled from place to place. They needed a food source they could take with them. Something nutritious that would keep well.

But now, some yogurt science, because there's some cool stuff going on in yogurt!

Cool Things Living in Our Intestines

You may not know that yogurt is alive! Yogurt contains billions of bacteria.

That's why it says "**live and active cultures**."

Don't worry. Yogurt bacteria are healthy bacteria. To make yogurt, add these bacteria to milk. The bacteria feast on the sugar in the milk and turn it into lactic acid in a process called fermentation.

This acid makes milk tart and thick. When milk is warm, the bacteria will thrive. The milk curdles, the bacteria multiply, and after several hours, you have yogurt!

Your intestines are filled with bacteria as well—3–4 pounds' worth! But don't rush to call the doctor. Most of the bacteria in your gut aids in digestion. If your gut contains the wrong kind of bacteria, you won't feel well.

The good bacteria in yogurt helps your digestive system work properly. By eating yogurt, you get more good bacteria into your gut to get rid of the bad bacteria and keep the balance.

So how did the herdsmen figure this out?

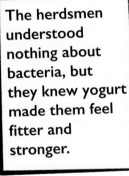

The herdsmen understood nothing about bacteria, but they knew yogurt made them feel fitter and stronger.

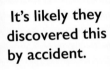

It's likely they discovered this by accident.

But they did understand the basic process for making yogurt. They experimented with milk from different animals. They strained it to make it even thicker.

And of course, they had to give it a name!

The word *yogurt* comes from the Turkic word "yoğurmak," which means to thicken or curdle.

They also made yogurt even more portable. They mixed it with wheat or barley, dried it in the sun, and rolled it into small balls that were perfect for long trips. The original snack pack!

These early travelers transported their yogurt knowledge through many parts of Asia, India, and Europe. As a result, yogurt became one of the most widely consumed foods in the world.

THE MIRACLE CURE FOR EVERYTHING

The spread of yogurt couldn't have come at a better time. Many people in ancient times were interested in how to stay healthy. They knew there was a connection between their health and what they ate.

The ancient Greeks saw yogurt as a miracle food. They believed there wasn't any problem with the body it couldn't solve.

You have to **eat it!**

But it wasn't just the Greeks who understood how great yogurt was. In the 9th century, Hunayn ibn Ishaq, the father of Islamic medicine, wrote:

Yogurt can **cure diarrhea, cool the blood, and** give **a healthy color to the skin.**

People didn't know about bacteria yet, so no one knew why yogurt worked. They just knew it did.

Why does this work?

No idea.

It wasn't until many centuries later that someone finally discovered the secret.

THE YOGURT SUPERHERO
Eli METCHNIKOFF

In the early 1900s . . .

What are you looking at, Dr. M.?

Bacteria from my **intestines!**

Sounds (ugh!) fascinating!

I am looking at something of **great importance!**

See? **Good bacteria! Not bad stuff!**

Yeah? So what?

The good bacteria come from the yogurt I ate this morning!

All this squirmy stuff can only mean one thing . . .

15

After having solved the mystery of yogurt, Dr. Metchnikoff died in 1916 at the age of seventy-one. Might his life have been shorter if he hadn't eaten yogurt? No one will ever know!

Yogurt Gets Sugary and Colorful

For years the production of yogurt remained the same as it did when those first herdsmen discovered it. However, within the past century, yogurt manufacturers began mass-producing yogurt for grocery stores. And they also wanted to improve the taste to get people to eat more of it.

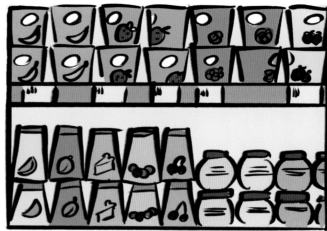

The herdsmen who discovered yogurt wouldn't recognize today's yogurt. Yogurt has sugar (sometimes a lot), artificial flavors, and artificial colors. Some yogurt has fruit mixed in, or comes with granola as part of the package. Some even have sprinkles! Just like breakfast cereal, yogurt became less healthy.

Breakfast cereal and yogurt are quick and easy breakfasts.

But sometimes you want something a little more substantial . . .

Something like WAFFLES!

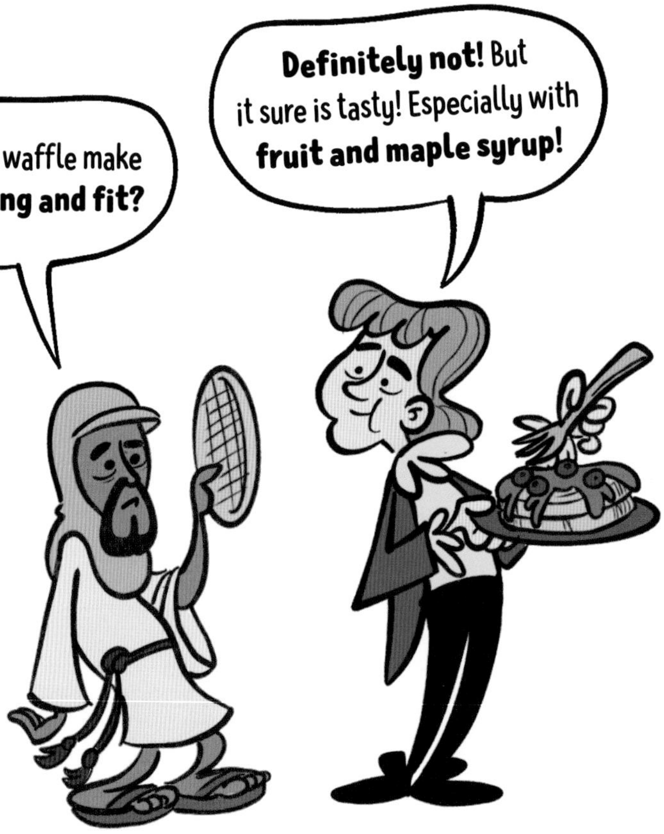
Will this waffle make me **strong and fit?**
Definitely not! But it sure is tasty! Especially with **fruit and maple syrup!**

The Birth of Waffles

The ancient Greeks were the first to make something like the waffle we know today. They made a flat cake out of flour and water and called them obelios.

The Greeks placed the dough between two metal plates and cooked them over the fire, flipping them once to cook both sides.

Obelios were just flour and water—no syrup or butter or anything like that. And they were dense, not fluffy. But people ate them like that for centuries.

In the 14th century, much of Europe (The Netherlands, Belgium, Luxembourg, and parts of France and Germany), turned their obelios into works of art. They crafted designs on the metal plates—family crests, landscapes, and other artistic designs—that got pressed into the waffles as they cooked.

An unknown craftsman in the 12th century made an iron with the deep honeycomb pattern that we use with waffles today. Gradually those thin obelios wafers became known as waffles.

Walfre means "honeycomb" in French!

Waffles Hit the Streets

Waffles got even better! During the 15th and 16th centuries explorers brought back spices, such as cinnamon, ginger, and nutmeg. Waffle cooks added some of these spices.

Cinnamon

nutmeg

ginger

These same cooks also learned that if you added cream, honey, and butter to waffles, they became sweeter and fluffier—and more delicious! And so waffle fever grew and grew.

Life was good in Renaissance Europe if you liked waffles. Waffle vendors on every corner sold as many waffles as a person could eat. And who wouldn't want to eat a waffle on the go?

People got their money's worth —these waffles were the size of pizzas! No toppings, though. They were eaten plain.

But only after noon! Waffles were afternoon snacks.

Waffle selling got competitive. In France, waffle sellers fought over the best places to sell. It got so bad that King Charles IX decreed that they had to stay six feet apart. An early form of social distancing!

6 ft.

Waffles and Maple Syrup
(a sweet story)

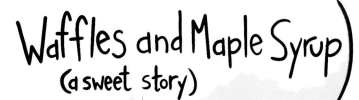

Waffles were so beloved by the Dutch that they brought them along to their colonies in New York's Hudson Valley in the 1600s.

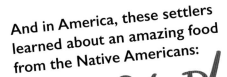

And in America, these settlers learned about an amazing food from the Native Americans:

MAPLE SYRUP!

The Native Americans cut into the trunk of a tree and gathered the sap that dripped out.

Then they boiled the water out of the sap to create syrup.

The early settlers made one significant change. Instead of cutting into the trunk, they bored a hole into the tree and put a spout in it to collect the sap in buckets (this is called tapping, and is still done today).

They then boiled the sap in a series of vessels until it became thick and sweet, much like the maple syrup we enjoy today.

I drink it!

Waffles Become The Life of The Party

Thomas Jefferson was a huge fan of democracy . . . and waffles.

He discovered how tasty waffles were in France while serving as secretary of state. In 1792, he brought back four waffle irons he bought in Amsterdam.

He hosted "waffle frolics"—big waffle shindigs. Guests pigged out on waffles with all sorts of toppings, from maple syrup to kidney stew.

OLD-SCHOOL WAFFLE RECIPE

- A small amount of butter
- flour
- milk
- yeast (baking powder is more common today)
- no sweeteners!

1. Smear the waffle iron with pork fat so the batter doesn't stick.

2. Cook the waffle over an open fire.

3. Turn it over carefully.

WAFFLE MAKERS BEWARE!

Until the mid-1800s, only the brave made waffles.

This is Benjamin. He's going to make his first waffle.

Waffle irons were very heavy and hard to handle, as well as extremely hot.

Plus, it was easy to burn waffles by cooking them too long.

And he could drop them in the fire by accident!

Something had to be done. People wanted waffles, but they wanted an easier way to make them.

23

In 1869

Cornelius Swartwout

came up with a solution! He created a useful invention— the stovetop waffle iron.

This new device allowed you to fill the iron over a wood stove and turn the waffles without getting burned. Plus, no one would drop a waffle in the fire.

This basic design led to the first electric waffle iron in 1918. Now people didn't need a stove. This was around the time that American families began filling their homes with kitchen appliances.

By the mid-1930s, every respectable kitchen had a waffle iron handy. And many people cooked them right at the breakfast table!

The frozen waffle was invented in 1950. This required only an appliance that everyone had— toasters. Today, most waffles eaten in the US come out of the freezer, and aren't made from scratch.

And why not? Finally, waffles didn't take much time to prepare. They were just like cereal and yogurt—a fast, convenient meal.

WAFFLES AROUND the WORLd

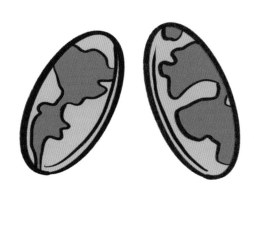

Stroopwafels (The Netherlands)

Bubble Waffles (China)

Pizzelle (Italy)

Pandan Waffles (Vietnam)

Hot dog Waffles (Canada)

Taiyaki (Japan)

LUNCH AND DINNER

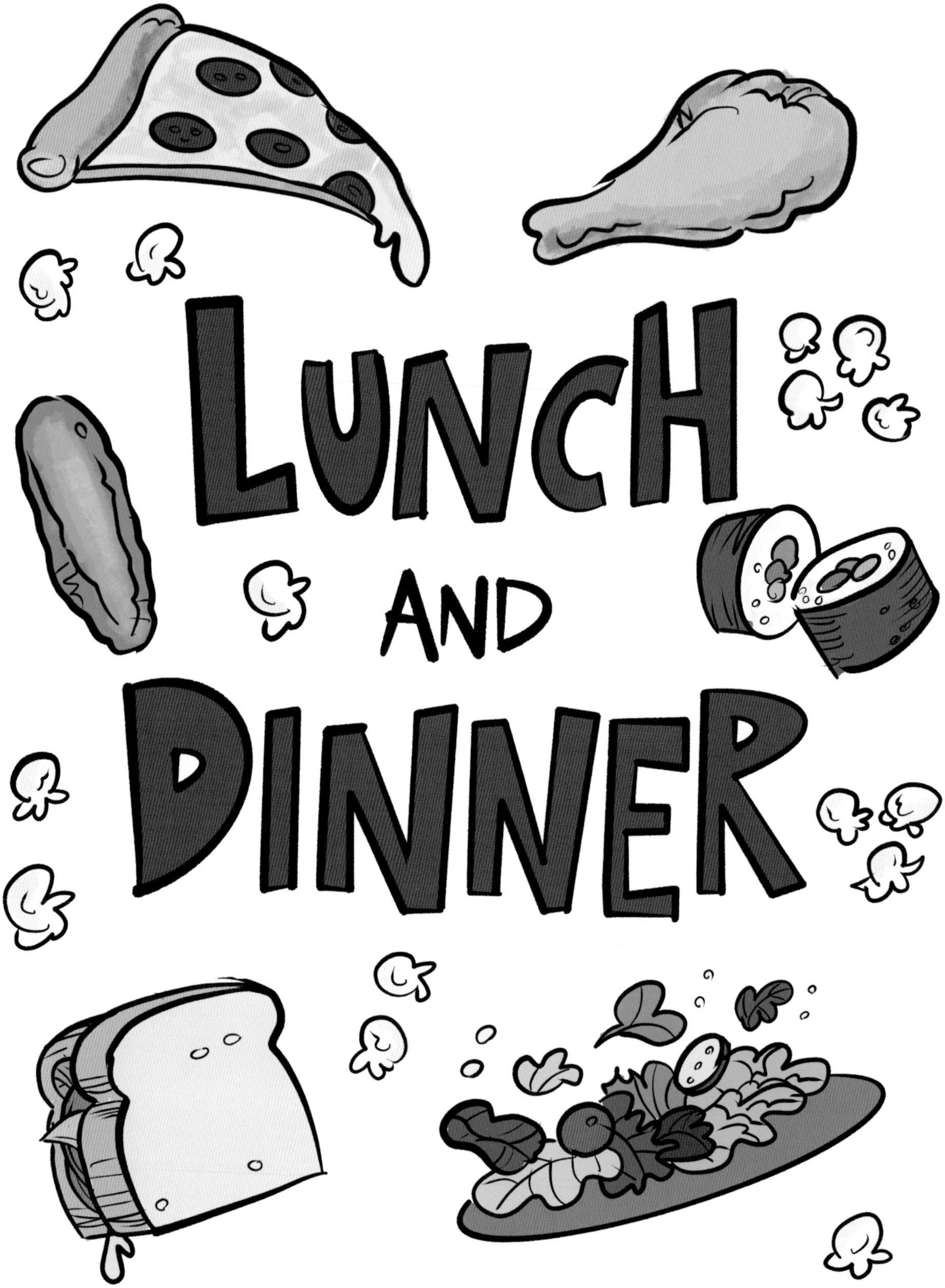

Winner, winner! LUNCH and DINNER!

Most days, you probably eat lunch or dinner around the same time. But in the distant past, as with breakfast, these meals had no set time. People ate when they were hungry. And they didn't have words for *lunch* or *dinner* yet.

Before electricity, people tended to eat in the daytime. Because guess what? It's hard to cook in the dark.

The concept of lunch appeared in the 17th century once people had regular work schedules. And later on, when people started working in factories, they ate in the middle of the day to sustain themselves. The lunch break became an established part of work.

Dinner as an evening meal began in the 19th century when people (men, primarily) went off to work and came home at predictable times. Dinner became the most important meal of the day, when everyone in the family was together after work and school.

For our first meal, let's start with pizza! How old are pizzas? And who invented them? And when could you start getting pizza delivered to your front door?

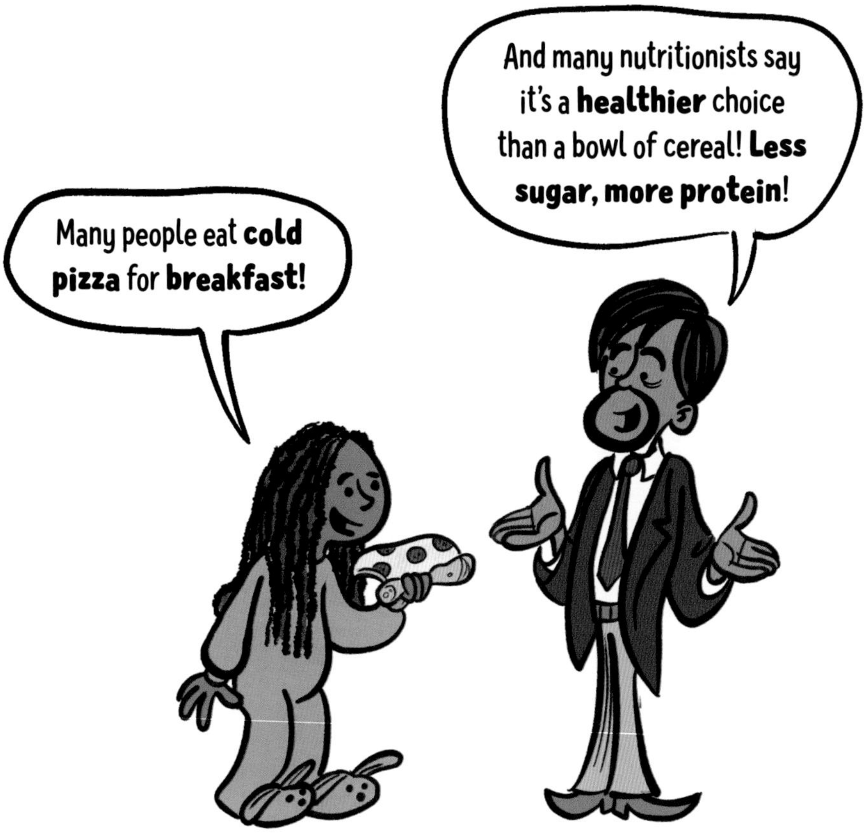
Many people eat **cold pizza** for **breakfast**!
And many nutritionists say it's a **healthier** choice than a bowl of cereal! **Less sugar, more protein**!

The Edible Plate

So what makes a pizza a pizza? Sauce? Pepperoni? Cheese? The first pizzas didn't have any of those toppings!

Early pizzas, like early waffles, were simple. People in ancient Greece mixed flour and water to form flatbreads that were cooked over a fire. As you might guess, they were pretty bland, so cooks added oil, honey, and herbs (basically anything handy) to make them taste better.

Pizzas were extremely handy for people who wanted to eat a meal on the go. It was a plate and a meal in one.

Naples Becomes the Place for Pizza

Medieval Italians added toppings like mushrooms and meat or fish to their pizzas. These early pizzas were filling meals that required only a few ingredients.

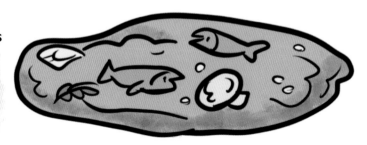

But still no cheese and tomato sauce! Pizza as we know it today started in Naples, Italy, in the 1700s.

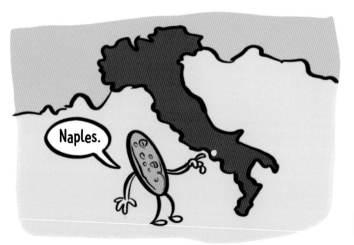

Naples.

In the early 1700s Naples wasn't a great place to live. Many people had moved there, more than the city could hold.

And many Neapolitans live in poverty.

Work is scarce.

We spend all day running around looking for work.

We need a cheap meal to eat on the go.

Who will come to our rescue?

Wait! Who's that?

THE PIZZA SUPERHERO
The PIZZA VENDOR!!

Get your pizza here!

The pizza vendor was a true pizza superhero for the working poor of Naples. He cooked pizzas on the street and sold slices to people on the go. Now they didn't have to stop and eat a meal. Pizza was an early fast food!

Pizza vendors cut slices according to what their customers could pay.

I earned a penny today. Can I get a slice?

Sure thing!

Rats! I need a better job.

I cleaned stables all morning!

And how did cheese and tomatoes get added? Here's how it might have happened . . .

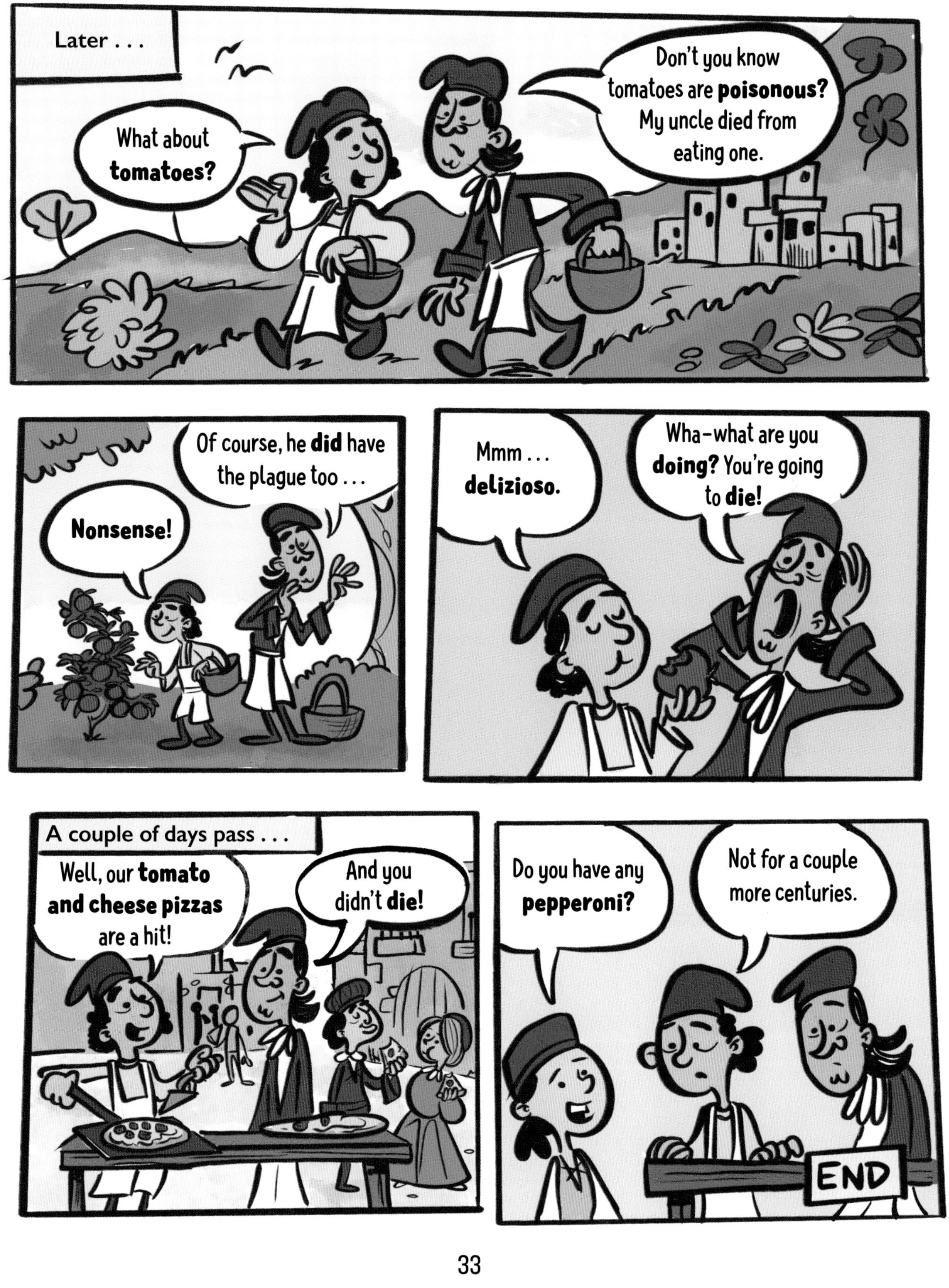
Later . . .
What about **tomatoes?**
Don't you know tomatoes are **poisonous?** My uncle died from eating one.
Of course, he **did** have the plague too . . .
Nonsense!
Mmm . . . **delizioso.**
Wha-what are you **doing?** You're going to **die!**
A couple of days pass . . .
Well, our **tomato and cheese pizzas** are a hit!
And you didn't **die!**
Do you have any **pepperoni?**
Not for a couple more centuries.
END

A Meal Fit For a Queen

Surprisingly, not everyone ate pizza. Wealthy people preferred to eat rich people's food that was expensive and took a long time to prepare.

But that all changed with QUEEN MARGHERITA!

Legend has it that Queen Margherita visited Naples with her husband in 1889. She grew tired of the fancy food she was served.

A local pizza chef made her three different pizzas. She didn't like the first two. Then the chef served her this . . .

Can you bring me some local cuisine? Not **royal food.**

TOMATOES, MOZZARELLA, + BASIL

She loved the pizza so much . . .

. . . that the pizza maker named it after her! You can still get margherita pizza today.

Pizza Prosperity in the States

So when did pizza make it to the United States? It took a while. Soldiers returning from World War II made pizza even more popular when they brought back a taste for it along with victory.

Before that, a wave of Italian immigrants brought recipes for pizza with them to America in the early 1900s.

Some of these immigrants opened pizza shops with huge coal-fired ovens that could heat up to 900 °. That's how they cooked pizza fast!

And they used an AMAZING INVENTION: CANNED TOMATO SAUCE!

Tomatoes were a popular topping, but at the time they weren't available year-round. Tomato sauce did the trick and became the popular pizza sauce it is today.

How To Toss Pizza Dough

Why should you toss pizza dough?

1. To get it to the size you want
2. To build a nice crust on the edges
3. To dry out the edges slightly to get a crispier crust

Step one: Spread the ball of dough with your hands to make a circle.

Step two: Slap the pizza dough back and forth between your palms to stretch it out.

Step three: Hold the dough on your palm and toss it in the air in a circular motion. Catch it on the way down.

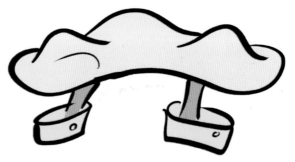

Step four: Eventually the "skin" will be so large you'll have to catch it with your fists. Keep tossing until it's stretched out as large as you want!

The Portable Pizza

For a long time if you wanted to eat pizza, you had to go to a restaurant and eat it there. Soon, pizzerias offered pizzas to go that hungry families could take home.

Then, In the 1950s, pizzerias began to deliver to your house. Many of them promised they would get their pizza to you in thirty minutes or it would be free.

Thus, pizza became a go-to choice for families who didn't want to cook but didn't want to go out for dinner, either. Today most people eat pizza at home instead of at a restaurant.

In 2001, a pizza was delivered to the International Space Station! It cost about $1 million to get it there. It wasn't cheap and fast, but nothing keeps pizza away from people—even astronauts!

An invention that led to even more home pizza consumption was

FROZEN PIZZA!

Crust baked first

Next the sauce is poured on top.

Cheese is designed to be frozen.

Frozen at −23°F.

Frozen pizzas are made entirely by machines.

Chances are you have a frozen pizza in your freezer—over two-thirds of Americans do.

But you have to cook it first!

PIZZA AROUND the WORLd

Pizza is so beloved that people eat it around the world. However, the toppings people like are different in each place, and depend on what's available in the culture of the people who eat them.

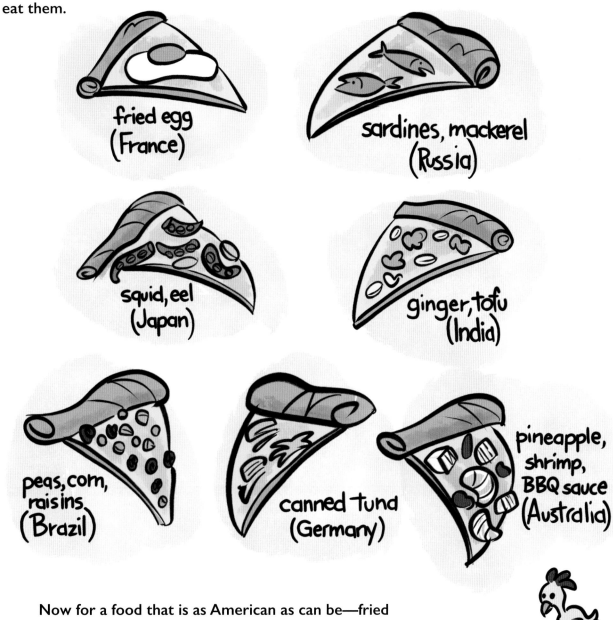

fried egg
(France)

sardines, mackerel
(Russia)

squid, eel
(Japan)

ginger, tofu
(India)

peas, corn, raisins
(Brazil)

canned tuna
(Germany)

pineapple, shrimp, BBQ sauce
(Australia)

Now for a food that is as American as can be—fried chicken. It's the food of picnics and the Fourth of July. It's greasy, crunchy, salty, and delicious. What more could you ask for?

39

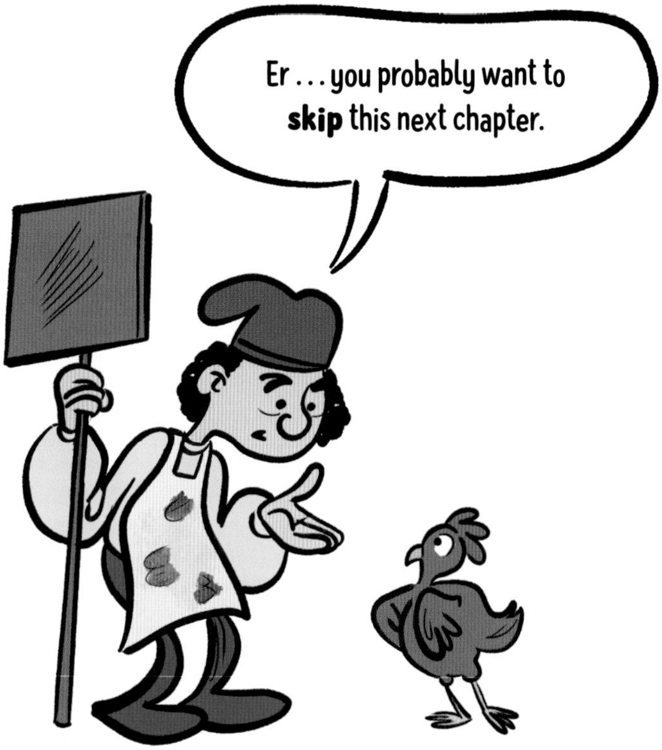
Er . . . you probably want to **skip** this next chapter.

Chickens Take Off

Around 1,500 BCE, people in Asia first started hunting chickens. Hunters lured chickens out of trees with rice.

FRIED CHICKEN

Then they found that once they caught them, chickens were easy to keep close to home. They couldn't fly well, so they didn't escape. People could get fresh eggs from them, too.

Chickens weren't food at first. They were more like highly respected pets.

The Egyptians hung chicken eggs in their temples to bring forth a river flood to help their crops grow.

Hey! Those are mine!

41

During the Roman Empire, generals watched a chicken before a battle. If a chicken ate a lot, the army would win.

However, like other cultures had already discovered, these Romans also knew that chickens were delicious.

One possible origin for fried chicken is Scotland. The Scots had been frying food since the Middle Ages. And when they came to the Americas in the 1700s, they brought their chicken-frying techniques with them.

Some of these Scottish people became landowners and made money growing crops like cotton, which made them wealthy. Growing and harvesting cotton was hard work. Those landowners bought enslaved Black people to do all that work for them.

Enslaved people also worked in the enslaver's house, and some of them were cooks. The cooks made fried chicken because the landowners wanted it. They drew on their chicken frying knowledge from their home countries (mainly West Africa) to perfect the recipe.

Enslaved people sometimes kept a few chickens in their quarters. They created their own fried chicken using the rations of cornmeal and pork fat they were given to survive.

Still, because they didn't have a whole lot of chickens, fried chicken was only for special occasions, such as gatherings after Sunday church services.

How to Make Old-School Fried Chicken

Making fried chicken then was way more difficult than it is today! Here's Betty. She's going to make fried chicken.

First, Betty has to catch and kill a chicken.

Next, she plunges the chicken into hot water to loosen the feathers.

Then she plucks the feathers.

She'll cut the chicken into large pieces.

She'll brine it in buttermilk for a while.

After brining, she'll coat it in flour and spices.

Finally, she fries it in a cast-iron skillet filled with melted lard (animal fat).

Betty is finally ready to enjoy the fried chicken that took her hours to prepare. That is, if she can stay awake!

After the Civil War, fried chicken became a way that freed Black people, and especially Black women, gained financial independence.

THE FRIED CHICKEN SUPERHEROES
THE WOMEN OF GORDONSVILLE, VIRGINIA

Our fried chicken is divine! And that's the truth!

We should start selling it!

But there aren't enough people in Gordonsville to sell to! Who would buy our chicken?

What they're saying makes sense.

Let's do it! Our chicken might be the ticket to the good life! But where could we sell it?

I've got it! Let's sell it at the train station!

That's a good idea!

And so they cooked up a bunch of fried chicken and took it to the train station at Gordonsville, where hungry people stopped all day.

They carried the fried chicken on their heads so the passengers could see it.

These people love our fried chicken.

That's because they don't serve good food on these trains!

Soon their chicken became the talk of the trains.

Gordonsville's clear out of your way!

I know! But have you had the fried chicken there?

We've done a heap of business here!

You said it!

These women paved the way for other formerly enslaved women to earn an income selling food. Some opened up their own restaurants in the South around the turn of the century. And many had a fried-chicken special on Sunday.

The Shoebox Lunch Helps Out

At these restaurants, people could pick up a shoebox lunch. It consisted of a piece of fried chicken, a piece of fruit, and a napkin.

A shoebox lunch was a perfect meal for people traveling or on a lunch break because it was very portable and could be eaten hot or cold. And no utensils were needed!

Because Black people were not welcome at many places in the South for a long time after they were freed, the shoebox lunch made travel possible. They could safely eat meals on the go.

WHITES ONLY

Fried chicken quickly became a popular food in America in the 20th century. And then it spread around the world!

FRied Chicken ARouNd The WORLd

Fried chicken isn't just eaten by Americans! Fried chicken restaurants have spread worldwide. In Japan, millions of people celebrate Christmas by ordering fried chicken takeout.

People have been eating chickens and frying foods for years, and developing their own ways to make it. So each culture's fried chicken is different! Here's a look at fried chicken in other cultures:

chicken lollipops
(India)

chongqing chicken
(China)

pollo frito
(Mexico)

ayam goreng
(Indonesia)

chicken kiev
(Ukraine)

pica pollo
(Dominican Republic)

schnitzel (Austria)

NEXT UP: SANDWICHES!

THE SANDWICH

PEOPLE LOVE SANDWICHES! In fact, Americans eat 300 MILLION sandwiches EVERY DAY!

Life Before Sandwiches

In the mid-1700s, if you had asked someone for a sandwich, no one would have known what you were talking about.

*What's a **sandwich**?*

Does that have anything to do with the beach?

Or witchcraft?

Actually, people had been eating something like sandwiches for years—they just weren't called that. The earliest was created by a Jewish rabbi named Hillel the Elder—a "sandwich" to eat during Passover. A version of it is still eaten today.

Matzo, lamb, and bitter herbs.

And people in Greece and Turkey had been filling pitas with meat for centuries. This may have given a traveler named John Montagu an idea when he visited.

Hey! What's that?

John Montagu, the Earl of Sandwich

Montagu lived in the 1700s in England. More importantly, he was the 4th Earl of Sandwich. He was a politician, and he liked to work. A lot!

Work, work, work! All these legal briefs, government documents... who has time to **eat?**

Bring me something I can eat with one hand. **Nothing messy!** Something like this—

His servant brought out a slice of meat between two slices of bread. In just a few minutes . . .

THE SANDWICH WAS BORN!

This is **great!**

I can write and turn pages with one hand and hold lunch with the other!

Soon some of the Earl's friends came to visit.

Egad! What is Montagu **eating?**

I don't know, to be sure!

Who knew you could eat a meal without seventeen utensils and ten plates?

Or twelve courses!

We could eat one of those . . . whatever they are . . . and play cards without having to get up from the table!

Yes! Or pick our nose with one hand and eat a meal with the other!

We'll have . . . the same as Sandwich!

Yes! The same as Sandwich!

The name "sandwich" stuck. And soon Britain was gripped by . . .

Sandwich Mania!

The British couldn't get enough sandwiches. They ordered sandwiches in pubs and restaurants, even though potato chips wouldn't be invented for another eighty years.

And they added all kinds of ingredients. Almost anything could be added to a sandwich.

LOBSTER

OYSTERS

ASPARAGUS

WATERCRESS

EGG

Sandwiches in America

People in America loved sandwiches too! However, the colonists weren't satisfied with small sandwiches. They liked them . . .

BIGGER AND BIGGER!

And Americans liked to name their sandwiches too.

reuben

hoagie

muffaletta

By the 1920s everyone in America was eating sandwiches—rich and poor, young and old, at home and at work.

They were also handy to take on trips on trains and boats and became a popular picnic food. They were easy to prepare and sturdy enough to pack.

And once sliced bread was invented in the 1920s, kids could make a quick, filling lunch by themselves. No knives or hot stoves needed!

I'm making a marshmallow, jam, and cookie sandwich!

SANdwicheS ARound the WoRLd

CHIP BUTTY (ENGLAND)

- buttered bread
- brown sauce
- mayo, ketchup, or malt vinegar
- french fries (or chips, as they call them in England.)

BANH MI (VIETNAM)

- baguette
- paté
- cilantro
- cucumber
- pickled veggies
- pork sausage

FALAFEL (MIDDLE EAST)

- diced cucumber
- onion
- tomatoes
- tahini
- falafel (fried chickpea + herb balls)
- pita

REUBEN (U.S.)

- rye bread
- 1,000 island dressing
- sauerkraut
- Swiss cheese
- corned beef

Do You Know What Goes Well With A Sandwich? A PICKLE!

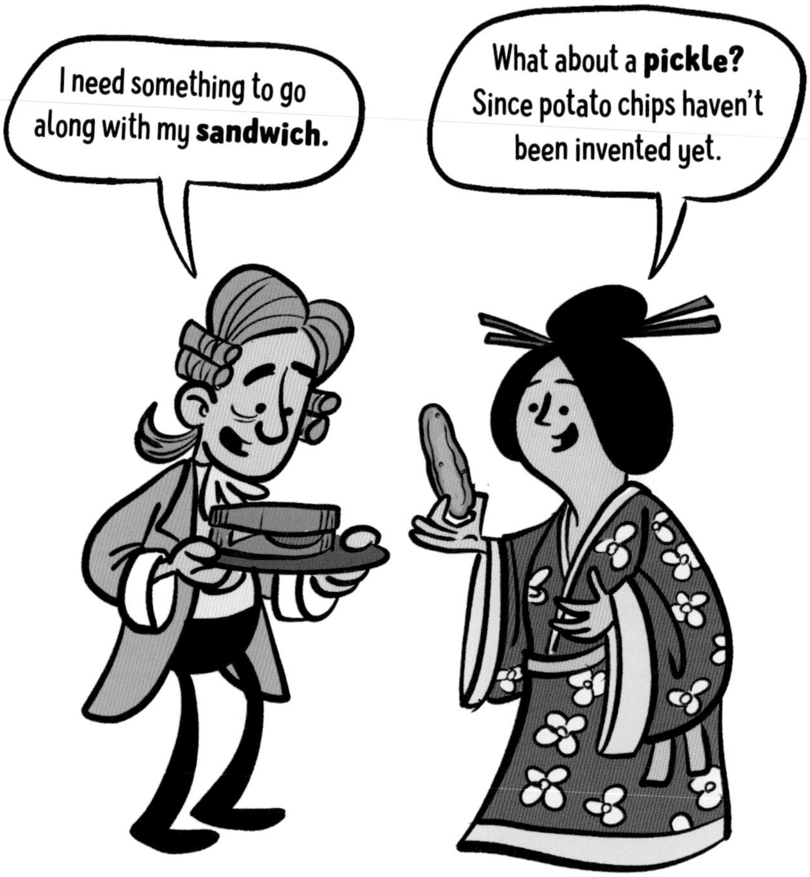
I need something to go along with my **sandwich.**
What about a **pickle?** Since potato chips haven't been invented yet.

PICKLES

People in many places have been making pickles for ages. People in China were making pickles 9,000 years ago. Not just because they tasted good.

Pickles are popular! Americans eat 20 billion pickles every year.

HOW TO PICKLE

A pickle is a perishable food (like a vegetable) soaked in a solution of some sort to preserve it for long periods. Foods like veggies spoiled very quickly, and pickling solved this pickle of a problem.

I really like cucumbers.

So do I! But they don't last!

There are two common ways to pickle food.

SALT PICKLING

The salt activates lactic acid, which preserves the cucumbers.

mix of water and salt

Use good quality salt

You can add spices like dill, pepper, and garlic to both!

Salt pickles can be eaten the next day.

VINEGAR PICKLING

solution of vinegar and water

Vinegar, with its high acidity, prevents the growth of microbes.

Vinegar pickles are ready to eat in a month.

Pickles can be stored at room temperature and don't spoil for a long time if they remain in the pickling solution. The salt also hardens pickles and makes them crisp.

People use pickling to store foods that could go bad. If they pickle crops after the harvest, they can eat them through the winter.

CRUNCH!

Almost every ancient culture, from Japan to Africa, used pickling. In many cultures people served pickles at every meal. That's because pickles were not only tasty, but also had impressive health benefits.

They aid digestion!

They give you beautiful skin!

They make Caesar's army strong!

Galen, 2nd cent. BCE

Cleopatra, 1st cent. BCE

Caesar, Same time period

PiCKLeS ARoUNd The WoRLd

Cucumbers are not the only pickles! You can pickle lots of foods, especially vegetables. And people do just that.

kimchi (Korea)

tomatoes (Russia)

sauerkraut (Eastern Europe)

eggs (Great Britain)

turnips (Lebanon)

radish (Japan)

eggplant (Italy)

mango (Hawai'i)

Pickles Come To America

The first pickles traveled to America with Christopher Columbus.

The world and pickles are not flat!

Not only did pickles keep well, but they had a lot of vitamin C. This prevented scurvy, a disease common among sailors.

bloody gums

tired →

spots →

You need pickles!

However, Columbus wasn't much of a giver. He was more of a taker. He brought back potatoes, pineapples, and other foods from the New World, but kept all the pickles—and how to make them—for himself and his crew.

Arrivederci!

Thanks for the potatoes!

The Dutch brought the pickling process to what is now Brooklyn, New York, in 1659. They not only made pickles, but sold them on the street.

Pickles!

Boudewijn's PICKLES

Most colonists grew and stored much of their own food at home. They didn't have refrigerators. They worked hard to grow fruits and vegetables and save them for the winter.

And they also built food cellars to provide a dry cool place to store food until they needed it.

Did you know that people once used an early form of plastic wrap to store food?

pig bladder (early plastic wrap)

vinegar, water, + cucumbers

glazed crock

But preserving food took time, and didn't always work. People didn't know how to recognize stored food that had gone bad. As a result, people got sick from eating food that looked good, but wasn't.

I wonder what happened?

UUGH

In 1858 a man named John Mason found a solution—the mason jar!

JOHN MASON
(A JARRING STORY)

only 26!

His jar had a self-sealing, airtight lid that kept air and bacteria out of the jar.

screw top

rubber gasket

Mason jars made preserving food easier and more reliable (so, fewer illnesses and deaths). They also led to jarred pickles in grocery stores, because pickles were now easy to mass produce. People didn't need to pickle their own cucumbers (although they could).

Pickles were about to get even more popular! In the late 1800s and early 1900s, Jewish immigrants from Europe brought their love of pickles with them to their new home. Some of them opened up delicatessens in New York City.

The delicatessen owners offered pickles as a free side with a sandwich. Customers fished them right out of the barrel! You can find pickle barrels in delis to this day.

TYPES OF PICKLES

Dill-uses dill in the fermentation process

Kosher- pickled in salt, dill, and (most importantly) garlic.

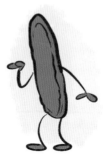

Sour- brine doesn't contain vinegar-just water, salt, and spices

Sweet - sugar added to brine

Bread and butter- thinly sliced, with sweet onion

Hungarian - uses bread to start fermentation

Candied- packed in a sweet syrup

Cinnamon-with cinnamon sticks and red hot candies

There's another food that first involved pickling... SUSHI!

A Fishy Problem

In Asia, back around 700 CE, people caught fish in different ways. Sometimes it was as simple as picking up fish after flooding rice fields.

People along the Mekong River in what is now Laos, China, and Thailand, developed a particularly ingenious way. They used cormorants, birds that lived on fish.

Fishermen tied them to ropes and put a small rope around their necks. The cormorants could swallow small fish, but not the large ones. The fishermen pulled the big fish out of the birds' mouths and sent them back in for more.

But they had a problem. Fish spoiled quickly and they needed a way to preserve it.

URP!

We'll have to eat all of these today!

How To Preserve Fish
THE ANCIENT WAY
(if you start now, it will be ready next year)

Many fishermen dried their fish. But there was another way that people had been using since the 3rd century BCE that—eventually—led to the development of sushi.

1. Remove the scales and guts and pack the fish with salt.

2. Put the fish in a barrel with more salt. Let it sit for six months.

Stones weigh it down

Salt destroys bacteria and softens bones

3. Remove the fish and rinse it off. Place it in a new barrel with cooked rice.

Still weighed down!

rice ferments and creates lactic acid, which preserves the fish

4. Let it sit for another six months. After that it will be good for decades!

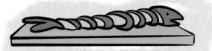

5. Slice the fish as thin as you can. Meshiagare! (ready to eat).

When they finally opened the barrel, the smell was terrible!

But the fish tasted great.

The rice, on the other hand, did not. They threw it away.

Sushi was made this way for many years. In the 1800s sushi was a popular dish in busy Edo (modern-day Tokyo). People would go to market and buy a sushi snack from people carrying it around in boxes. But sushi sellers needed a way to make sushi faster.

THE SUSHI SUPERHERO... YOHEI HANAYA!

People love my sushi. But it takes so long to make. Plus, I always smell like (ugh!) **dead fish!** My wife won't go near me!

There has to be a **better** way.

Something faster. And that **smells better.**

I know! What if I just used raw fish? And fresh rice with vinegar?

I could make sushi in minutes! Well, here goes nothing . . .

Yohei took a slice of raw fish and put it on a ball of rice soaked in vinegar. It took no time to prepare!

And Yohei's sushi—called nigiri sushi—was born! But would it be a hit?

And so . . .

Yohei's sushi is **unreal!**

Yeah, and you can get **tuna, mackerel, eel** . . . all **made to order**

It even **smells** fresh!

Yohei's sushi became an early fast food for people in busy Edo. He opened a sushi stand instead of carrying it around.

Yohei transformed sushi. His new sushi was quick. And it sold well.

SUSHI BLOWS UP!

Pretty soon it was easy to get sushi anywhere in Edo. It was a quick meal for people on the go.

It was easy to tell where the best sushi was. Since people ate with their fingers, the vendors hung a strip of cloth in front of the stand so people could wipe off their hands.

The dirtier the cloth, the better the sushi.

SUSHI ON A ROLL IN AMERICA

Although sushi could be found here and there in America, it really arrived when Japanese immigrants opened up sushi restaurants in California in the 1960s. At first, many non-Japanese Americans didn't like the idea of eating raw fish. No nigiri sushi!

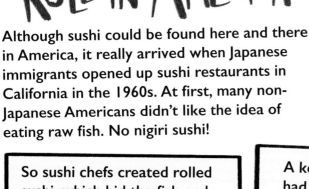

So sushi chefs created rolled sushi, which hid the fish and seaweed (and anything else Americans didn't like) inside the roll.

A key invention was the California roll, which had cooked crab and avocado in it instead of raw fish. It was a big hit.

By the 1980s, sushi restaurants had spread across America.

66

If you want to start making sushi, you can't just start tomorrow. It's a long process!

HOW TO BECOME A SUSHI CHEF

(It takes longer than you think.)

Here's Himari. She's training to become an itamae (a sushi chef) in Japan. In the past, Himari wouldn't be able to. Sushi was believed to be a man's job. One reason: women's hands were thought to be warmer, which would ruin the sushi. But Himari isn't afraid of succeeding in a man's world!

Becoming a sushi chef isn't for the faint of heart or those with a busy schedule. Himari will spend the next ten years training!

For the first two years, Himari will learn how to cook rice and season it, getting the mixture of vinegar, sugar, and salt just right.

Once she masters rice, she'll become a wakiita, who works next to the chef, preparing fish and slicing ginger and scallions.

There are lots of skills Himari will have to master:

I'm already tired!

Buying fish.

Calculating a customer's bill in her head.

Carry the two . . .

Packing sushi so it doesn't fall apart.

Making sushi that is uniform in size.

Whoops!

Developing a recipe for nikiri, the chef's special sauce. A closely guarded secret!

Sharpening her knives daily.

After a few years spent perfecting her skills, Himari can earn the title of itamae, and can now stand in front of the cutting board and serve customers.

And after ten full years of training, Himari officially becomes a sushi chef who can own her own sushi bar.

So maybe you're in the mood for something else healthy.

WHAT ABOUT A SALAD?

SALAD

The Start of Salad

Salads have been around since ancient times. To make one, people only had to gather some wild lettuce, add some oil, vinegar, and herbs, and they had a meal! No recipe needed.

No cooking was needed either, so people didn't have to start a fire. It was a nutritious time-saver.

In ancient Greece and Rome, wealthy people could afford to have people grow their greens and have servants prepare them. But peasants had to forage in the woods and eat what they could find.

Back then salad greens were dipped in the dressing. Eating utensils hadn't been invented yet!

That's **poison hemlock!**

Too big!

Salads Get Bigger and Better

Around the time of the Renaissance, chefs experimented with adding other vegetables, like asparagus, green beans, and cucumber, with different types of lettuce.

Eventually, people caught on: salads are awesome! The Renaissance was the heyday of the salad. All the great European kings were scarfing them down.

But being rich, they couldn't be satisfied with regular old salads. Their cooks made fancy salads. Salads included as many as thirty-five ingredients. It was a way for cooks to show off their skills.

There was no refrigeration at this time, so everything had to be harvested close to the time it was eaten.

And during the 14th century, the fork became a common eating utensil, making salads easier to eat.

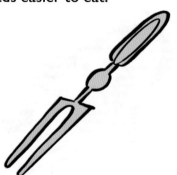

Hurry up!

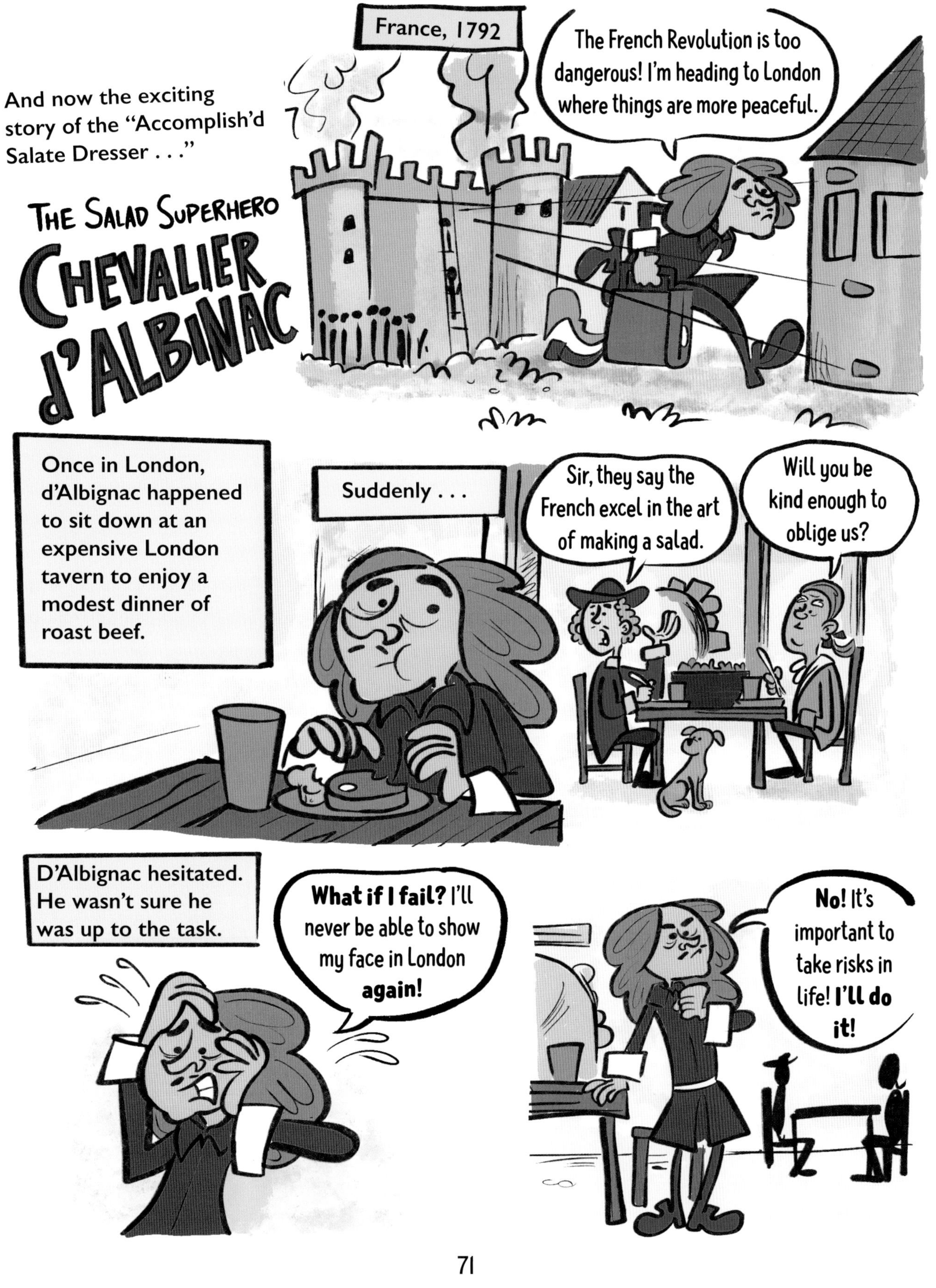
And now the exciting story of the "Accomplish'd Salate Dresser . . ."
THE SALAD SUPERHERO
CHEVALIER d'ALBINAC
France, 1792
The French Revolution is too dangerous! I'm heading to London where things are more peaceful.
Once in London, d'Albignac happened to sit down at an expensive London tavern to enjoy a modest dinner of roast beef.
Suddenly . . .
Sir, they say the French excel in the art of making a salad.
Will you be kind enough to oblige us?
D'Albignac hesitated. He wasn't sure he was up to the task.
What if I fail? I'll never be able to show my face in London again!
No! It's important to take risks in life! I'll do it!

He approached the table, added a little bit of this, a little bit of that, and created a historic salad.

By Jove!

Jolly good!

He was soon invited to dress a salad at one of the best houses in Grosvenor Square. His skills had made him famous.

He carried around a case with his salad-making supplies so he was ready to make a salad at a moment's notice.

D'Albignac grew wealthy enough to purchase a carriage to travel between homes. He eventually moved back to France, living comfortably the rest of his life.

Salads are a great way to get enough vegetables.

These aren't **vegetables**?

If you make a salad like d'Albignac and add a bunch of different vegetables, you can get your daily recommended amount of several nutrients.

Like **vitamin A** and **vitamin C**!

HOW TO MAKE AN AMAZING SALAD

This is Maryam. She's going to make a tasty salad for lunch.

She's going start with dark greens such as arugula, spinach, and kale, which are packed with vitamins.

Then she's going to add other tasty, nutritious foods.

seeds

sprouts

olives
nuts

avocado

berries

Maryam also knows that many dressings, especially the creamy ones, are very unhealthy. You might as well just put ice cream on your salad.

That sounds **pretty good!**

She's going to make her own salad dressing using a recipe the ancient Greeks would have recognized: some olive oil, some garlic, some vinegar, and salt and pepper.

Or if you want to be healthier, just drizzle some lemon juice on top!

And Maryam is going to start a home garden and grow lettuce and vegetables. Many greens grow quite well in a variety of conditions, and it's cheaper to grow your own. All it takes is good dirt, sunshine, a little water, and Mother Nature does the rest.

Popcorn is old! The earliest known popcorn was discovered in a place called Bat Cave in New Mexico in 1948. Indigenous people popped it more than 5,000 years ago!

The ancient people in Central and South America ate a lot of popcorn. The Aztecs offered it to their god Opochtli, and they used it in ceremonial clothing like headdresses and garlands. Young Aztec girls even performed a popcorn dance!

How did they pop it? The most common way was to toss popcorn ears directly into the fire and gather the popped kernels as they scattered on the ground.

75

POPCORN IN THE UNITED STATES

The soil and climate in North America were perfect for growing all types of corn. Eventually, early settlers in the Southwest started growing popcorn. The way popcorn popped was part of its appeal— it was so exciting to cook.

OOH!

AAH!

People loved popcorn so much that they ate it just about any way they could. Here are some examples:

as cereal with milk and sugar

ground into flour for pancakes

a topping for soup

Naturally, people looked for a better way to cook it than throwing it in the fire. They didn't like burnt, smoky popcorn with dirt on it.

Popcorn?

A better method was to put the popcorn in a heavy frying pan with lard. But lard-flavored popcorn was pretty gross.

BLECH!

76

Then in the 1800s some popcorn enthusiasts developed an invention to make popcorn taste better: The Popcorn Popper!

THE POPCORN POPPER!

Add popcorn kernels.

Pop the kernels over a stove or fire.

Enjoy with butter, salt, or maple syrup!

And people didn't always have to make popcorn at home. It was sold just about anywhere, from drugstores, to carnivals, to circuses.

But there was a problem . . .

I love popcorn!

Me too! I just wish we could get it anywhere!

The park is too far away!

And I've been banned from baseball games for gambling!

Fortunately, one man had a solution to bring popcorn to where the people were!

THE POPCORN SUPERHERO CHARLES CRETORS!

Charles Cretors had already changed the industry in 1885 by popping popcorn with steam power. His pop-corn was tasty too—it was popped in a combination of butter and lard and seasonings.

However, his popcorn machine was stationary. He wanted to get popcorn to people on the streets.

In the late 1800s he invented a truly revolutionary machine—the popcorn wagon! It was easily pushed or pulled from place to place by hand or by horse.

But how?

And by the 1900s, popcorn vendors—and popcorn—were everywhere. And not just at special events. Anyone could buy popcorn while walking down the street.

If sales were slow in one area, the popcorn seller moved the wagon, maybe to a park or a political rally.

Popcorn vendors started raking in money.

POPCORN GOES TO THE MOVIES

At the start of the 1900s popcorn was easy to find. At ten cents a bag, everyone could afford it. And then . . .

MOVIES HAPPENED!!

Movies happened! People flocked to the theaters. Popcorn vendors sold to the large crowds that gathered outside. However, theater owners refused to let popcorn inside. Too messy!

TOO MESSY!

But once they realized how much money could be made from concessions, popcorn became the ultimate movie snack. To this day, theaters make more money from popcorn than movie tickets.

Popcorn Goes Home

However, in the middle of the 20th century, people stopped going to movies as much. Why? People bought televisions and stayed home. There was plenty of free entertainment on the small screen.

The popcorn industry quickly found a better way to pop popcorn than the old popcorn poppers.

The amazing invention was the electric air popper.

What can we do?

An idea just popped into my head!

The air popper used hot air instead of oil. The popcorn was much healthier.

With this invention, people began to eat popcorn in their homes (much of which ended up in the couch cushions).

You have to keep the lid on!

Today, most people cook popcorn in a microwave oven. Popcorn was very important in the development of this appliance! And the guy that figured it out was

POPCORN SUPERHERO

PERCY SPENCER!

Spencer discovered the power of microwaves when he stood in front of an early radar set.

The chocolate bar in his pocket melted.

Figuring he was on to something, Spencer developed the first microwave oven.

One of the first foods he proved this with was popcorn! He put popcorn kernels in a bag, added butter and seasoning, and soon had a delicious bag of popcorn

Mmm, not bad!

CHOMP CHOMP

CHOMP CHOMP

Heating leftovers is the most common use of the microwave, but making popcorn is a close second. Today 70 percent of popcorn is eaten at home. Popcorn went from being a food that people could only eat at home, to a food that was sold largely at events and in the streets, and back to our homes. That's quite a journey!

Why does popcorn pop?

Popcorn is composed of a hard, outer shell called the pericarp, which is filled with the germ and the endosperm, which contain starch.

pericarp

endosperm

germ

I can't take the pressure!

Whether heated by air or in oil, the water inside the kernel heats up and expands, creating pressure on the pericarp.

Eventually the outer layer gives way, and the water and starch quickly dry to create the white fluffy exterior.

POP!

Ahh! Relief.

Why doesn't all corn pop?

Because popcorn is the only corn that has a pericarp that traps the water. Steam passes right through the outer shell of other types of corn because it's too soft.

So that about covers it . . . oh, wait! We forgot about

DESSERT!

DESSERT

THE SWEET HISTORY OF DESSERT

We are hardwired to enjoy sweet food, and people have been enjoying simple "desserts" like fruit and honey for years.

For centuries people ate sweets along with their meal.

> Please pass the ham and cookies.

Eventually the French began to eat sweets between courses to cleanse the palate. Not too much, though! They didn't want to spoil their appetite.

> C'est terrible!

Starting in the 17th century, people ate a dessert at the end of the meal. The word "dessert" comes from the French word *deservir*, which means to clear the table.

Etiquette demanded that you change the napkins and tablecloth before the final course, which became dessert.

Let's dig into a few common desserts: Cake, ice cream, AND apple pie!

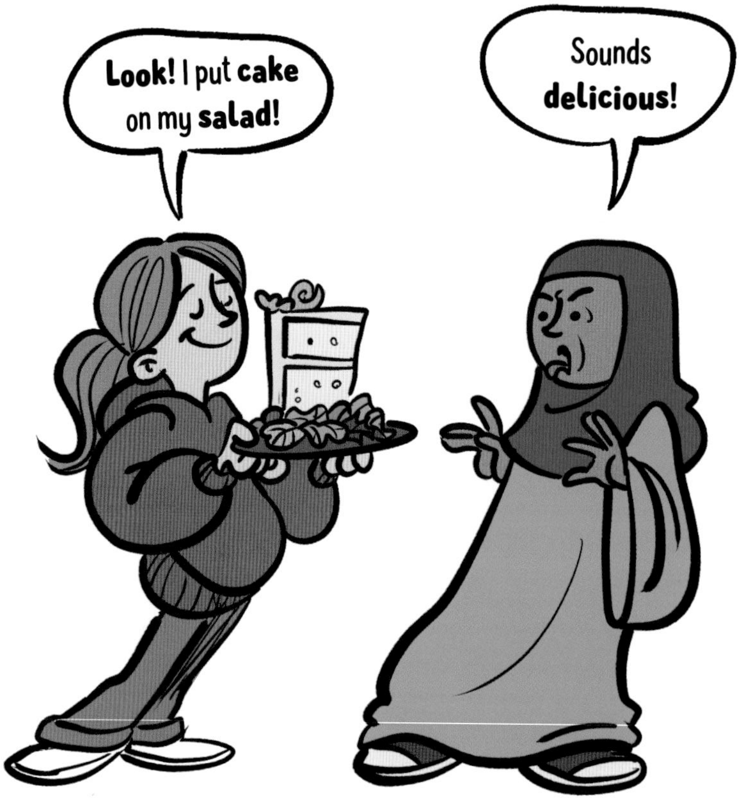

Look! I put cake on my salad!
Sounds delicious!

Cake Takes the Cake!

There's a good chance you ate cake this year. It might have been on your birthday. Or maybe someone else's birthday!

Cakes have been around since ancient times, but not like the cakes of today. For one thing, they didn't have sugar to sweeten them. They were also really coarse and more like bread.

However, cakes have been part of special occasions for centuries. The ancient Egyptians buried them with the dead to send them on their way to the afterlife.

no yeast!

honey added for sweetness

The ancient Greeks brought round cakes to the temple of Artemis, the goddess of the moon, as an offering. And they put candles on them.

One candle represented the light of the moon. When it was blown out, the smoke rose to the sky to carry a prayer to Artemis.

TEMPLE OF ARTEMIS
1,000 CUBITS

Blowing out candles? Sounds like a birthday cake! But this wasn't a birthday cake. Not quite yet.

Making OLD-SCHOOL CAKES was really hard!

By the 17th century, cake bakers made some important developments for cakes. Cooks discovered that adding sugar and butter into the batter made for a richer, tastier cake.

> Aye, but cakes are few and far between.

Why?

There weren't grocery stores where you could pick up butter and sugar like today, and many ingredients were expensive.

Folks might have a cow at home that could give them milk, but churning butter took hours of exhausting, boring work.

UGGH...

Sugarcane grew in tough stalks in places like Haiti. Because it was such hard work it was harvested by enslaved people and then shipped overseas. It was very expensive.

Just like with waffles, people also wanted spices like cinnamon, nutmeg, and ginger for their cakes. These were imported from the East Indies and weren't cheap either.

> Hurry up!

> I need cinnamon to finish my cake!

But people wanted cakes! Most women knew how to make cakes, but there were always a few unlucky souls who didn't. They needed

a cake superhero...

ELIZA LESLIE!

Somewhere in America in 1857...

Let's make a cake!

Good idea! What do we need?

Umm... Not sure.

Broccoli? Cabbage?

I know we need flour!

Great! How much do we need for one cake?

I don't know. Maybe the whole bag?

Do we need to bake it?

Umm... I think so?

If only there were some way to know!

Wait, who's that at the door?

89

Eliza Leslie bursts through the door!

Fear not! I'm here to save the day!

What is it?

My new cookery book. It's got recipes for plum cakes, cornbread cakes, rye battercakes, and shortcakes—

thirty types of cake!

I list the ingredients, with measurements in teaspoons and cups. No more wondering if a "handful" is too much if you have large hands!

I've even got recipes for icing so you can decorate your cakes too!

FWAP

At the end of a long day of mixing, beating, and cooking . . .

No problem! I'm going over to the Johnsons to teach them how to make goose pie!

Gosh, Miss Eliza! This cake turned out great!

Cake Baking Becomes a Cinch

People used to use a knife or a bundle of twigs to beat the eggs, and it took at least half an hour. And then they had to beat in the other ingredients.

Enter the baker's amazing invention—

THE WHISK!

Developed in the middle of the 19th century, the whisk reduced the time needed to whisk eggs and batter to a few minutes. Cooks, and their arms, were relieved.

There were several ingredients that made cake baking a breeze.

Sugar became very cheap in the 1800s due to mass production. It was something most people had on hand.

sugar

baking powder

Also, chemical rising agents, like baking soda and baking powder, were invented. They made cakes light and fluffy without all the effort of beating eggs.

Then came the electric oven at the beginning of the 1930s. At first, the gauge had only three settings: low, medium, and high. But now cooks could easily set a constant, steady temperature for a cake.

By the mid-20th century, electric ovens became a fixture in almost all kitchens. People could finally bake a cake at home!

HAPPY BIRTHDAY TO BIRTHDAY CAKES!

For centuries many people didn't know on what day they were born. It wasn't until the 1800s that the church started recording births.

It took a while for people to create cakes for birthdays. To find out why, we have to step back in time.

Germans in the late 1800s created the birthday celebration we know today. Children were presented with a cake with candles on the morning of their birthday.

People believed that on a child's birthday, they were easy prey for evil spirits. Parents left the candles burning all day to keep ghosts and goblins away.

The number of candles equaled the child's age, plus an extra candle. This represented the hope that the next year would go well.

At the time the cake was served, the child blew out the candles and made a wish, and kept it a secret so it would come true. (No gifts, just wishes.)

Cakes Become a Piece of Cake

People kept looking for even quicker ways to make cakes. After World War II, companies began to make cake mixes, which made baking a birthday cake quicker and easier. Fewer ingredients, less time.

Once cake making became easy, people turned their artistic side to frosting cakes. Cookbooks gave instructions on how to create flowers and piping out of frosting and write Happy Birthday in icing.

Cakes, birthday cakes especially, became a good way for mothers to show off their culinary skills.

Rats!

Is blowing out candles sanitary?

Scientists have found that blowing out candles does increase bacteria on the surface of the cake! However, you are more likely to get sick from eating too much cake than from eating germs on the cake.

After all, the birthday kid is blowing saliva (and maybe a few bits of pizza and pop) all over the top. You don't want to give a gift and get an illness.

BiRThdAY CAKES AROUND The WORLd

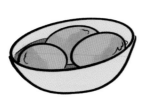

dumplings
served in syrup
(India)

rice and
vegetable cake
(Indonesia)

red tortoise
cake (symbolizing
long life and
success)
(Japan)

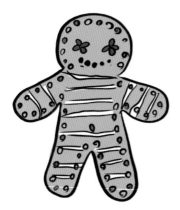

cake
shaped like a boy
or girl
(Denmark)

sweet rice
and bean cake on
the baby's 100 day
birthday
(Korea)

fruit pie
with the child's
name on it
(Russia)

OF COURSE YOU
KNOW WHAT
GOES WITH CAKE...

ICE CREAM!

People have loved cold treats for years. In the 1st century, Emperor Nero of Rome sent servants into the mountains to gather snow, which he then topped with wine or honey. The first snow cone!

What took you so long?

This wasn't ice cream, exactly—it didn't have cream. The first people to make a frozen confection with milk were the Chinese of the Tang dynasty (618–907 CE). They used fermented milk and ice, and added flour to make it thicker.

During the Middle Ages, people in Persia and Turkey enjoyed sharbat (sherbet) —a frozen drink made with ice and fresh fruit. Travelers likely brought the method for making sherbets back to Italy.

ITALY

Italians in the 1600s added sugar to the ice and fruit and called it sorbetto. And a sorbetto maker in Naples during the 17th century added milk, and made what we would call ice cream.

1ST

Ice Cream Becomes Cool

The Italians also figured out how to use ice or snow to freeze other substances. By immersing a container in a bucket of snow and then adding salt to the bucket, the freezing temperature of ice lowered, causing it to melt. This transferred heat away from the container and whatever was inside would freeze as the temperature dropped.

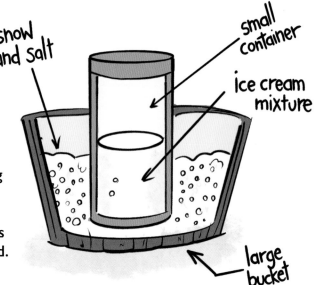

snow and salt

small container

ice cream mixture

large bucket

At first, people were suspicious of ice cream. They had never had cold food before. Food was either served at room temperature or hot from the oven.

It will freeze my insides!

And cause paralysis!

But making ice cream back then was

However, ice cream was so tasty they got over their fears. (Plus, nothing really bad happened).

I knew it was fine all along!

DiFFiCULT AND EXPENSiVE!

How to Make Old-School Ice Cream

This is Camille. She's going to make ice cream.

Ice wasn't readily available like it is today. It had to be taken from frozen lakes in large chunks.

The lack of refrigeration made it difficult to keep milk from going bad. People had to have a cow on hand and use the milk immediately.

Salt was expensive because it was mined in faraway places and making ice cream took a lot of it.

Sugar was another expensive import and was sold in large bricks that had to be broken up, pounded, and sifted before you used it.

Then Camille has to stir the ice cream constantly to keep it from freezing into a solid block of ice. The freezing process takes up to an hour and a half.

And it gets thicker!

Finally, it's ready! Because of all the time and effort, she'll have it only on special occasions. Plus, Camille and her friends have to eat it right away because they don't have a freezer.

Thus, in the 1700s only the wealthy, who could pay for the ingredients and servants to make it, enjoyed ice cream.

Bring me vanilla!

They even had a special fork just for ice cream.

But the wealthy weren't content to just eat ice cream. It had to be presented with style and flair.

Their cooks turned ice cream into a real art by pouring it into molds in the shape of animals, or vegetables like asparagus.

They also painted these creations with edible dyes to make them look as lifelike as possible. The cooks used some novel methods to make ice cream dyes. Green, for example, came from spinach juice or grass clippings.

QUACK!

And they experimented with unusual flavors!

WHICH OF THESE WAS NOT AN ICE CREAM FLAVOR?

parmesan   oyster   artichoke

tomato   celery   onion   avocado

A: They All Were!

Ice-cream making became much easier with the invention of a hand-cranked mechanism. In 1843, an American named Nancy Johnson filed a patent for the first ice-cream maker.

Believe it or not, it took a while for someone to invent the ice-cream scoop! It was invented by Alfred L. Cralle in 1897.

crank

dasher

salt

The Soda Fountain

This will give you your pep back!

In the late 1800s, the soda fountain helped make ice cream even more popular. Originally the soda fountain offered soda water (carbonated water) for medical purposes, like headaches and exhaustion. Not desserts!

One day a soda fountain owner was looking for a way to stand out from the others. He added ice cream and fruit flavoring to his soda water. The ice-cream soda was born!

The people that worked at soda fountains were called soda jerks. They weren't jerks (well, some of them might have been). They got their name from jerking back the lever to the soda fountain.

straw —
soda water
chocolate syrup
cherry
whipped cream
vanilla ice cream

They mastered cool tricks to amuse the customers, like flipping a scoop of ice cream in the air and catching it in the dish.

Ice Cream Goes to WAR!

Ice cream was also important to the morale of American troops in World War II. The US Navy was always looking for ways to keep sailors' spirits high. They wanted to send them something to remind them of home. So . . .

. . . they spent $1 million to send ice cream to the Western Pacific . . . on a barge!

an ice-cream barge!

The ice-cream barge was a floating ice-cream parlor that could make 1,500 gallons of ice cream in an hour. It served 800 million gallons of ice cream to sailors in the Pacific.

Pilots in the air force made ice cream in the sky. They filled a container with ice-cream mix and fastened it to the outside of the plane where it would get cold. The shaking of the plane churned the ice cream. Soon they had a tasty dessert. It's possible that ice cream helped the US armed forces win the war!

Time for one final food... APPLE PIE!

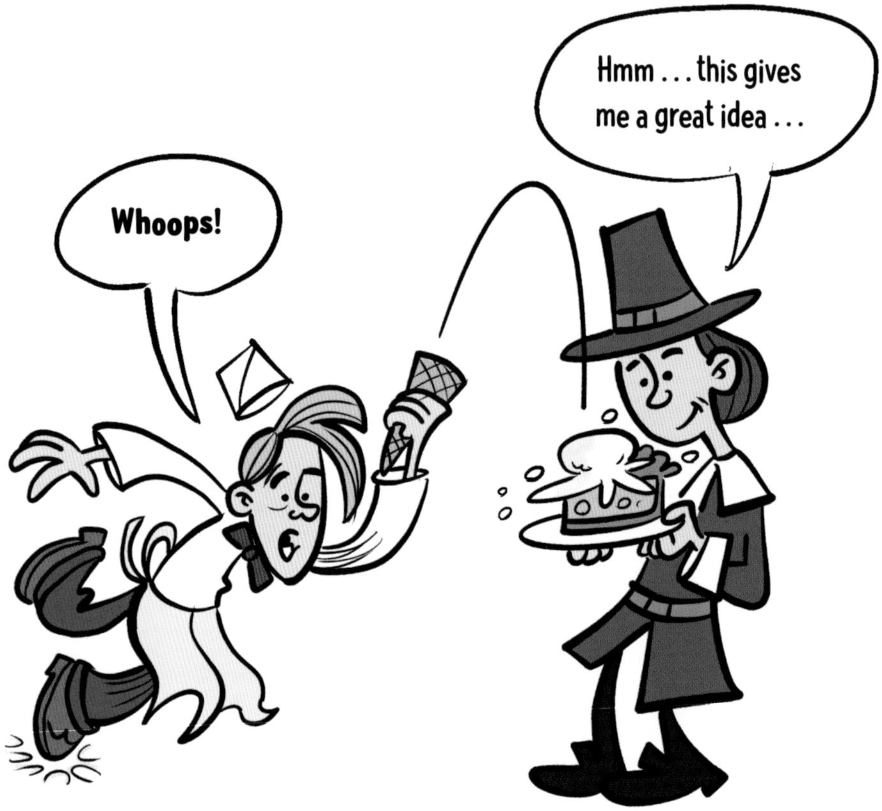
Whoops!
Hmm . . . this gives me a great idea . . .

Wild (for) Apples

All apples today come from the apple trees in the Tian Shan Mountains of Kazakhstan. Millions of years ago, early apples were wild in every sense of the word. And there were thousands of varieties.

Few were like today's apples, and most weren't very tasty. They came in all sizes, from small like marbles to as big as softballs. Some were red and yellow, some were purple, and some were blue.

Travelers passing through on the ancient Silk Road likely grabbed the few that were tasty to eat. As they traveled, they dropped the seeds, and apples spread throughout Asia and Europe.

Of course, people wanted to grow the apples they liked. How hard could it be? Just plant a seed from an apple and they'd have a tree full of them.

However, apples don't play by the rules. Even today if you plant an apple seed, the tree that grows may have different apples. And they might not taste very good. This frustrated people for a long time.

Yeehaw! Tasty apples are on their way!

old apple

new apple

Crafty Grafting

Around 2,000 BCE, people in China figured out the secret to growing the apples they liked: grafting!

These crafty horticulturists took a branch cut from the apple tree that had apples they liked . . .

. . . and placed it in a notch in a different apple tree. As the tree grew, the grafted branch grew the apples they wanted.

Grafting spread quickly, and everyone could grow the apples they liked the best. And as people explored the world, they brought these tasty apples with them to eat on the voyage. Why not? They kept well.

Some were good for baking,

and some were good for snacking.

Some were great for cider.

Apples could be used in lots of ways.

Apples in America

The earliest American colonists brought grafted apple trees over with them so they could enjoy their favorite varieties in their new home.

However, many of these trees did not grow well in their new climate. Winter killed a lot of them before they had a chance to grow.

Eventually, new varieties of apple trees grew, which could tolerate the new climate. The colonists also brought over honeybees in the 17th century.

The bees increased pollination—and apple production—dramatically. The colonists were finally able to grow apple trees.

And as these apple trees spread, new varieties appeared. Thanks to the honeybees, apple trees were pollinated from other apple trees. Apples can adjust and adapt, remember?

Using the science of grafting, the colonists experimented with creating different varieties of apples from those trees, and in doing so created delicious apples that could grow in the soil and climate of America.

As settlers moved westward, claiming land and building homes, planting an apple tree was a common way to stake their claim.

In fact, in Virginia, new landowners were required to plant an apple tree. Thus, there were apples aplenty in the colonies.

By 1800 America had 14,000 different varieties of apples, some with interesting names like Funkhouser and Father Abraham.

Shouldn't we have planted it outside?

I'm going to call this apple "booger breath."

And those that weren't eaten right away could be cooked and stored by a method called "sugaring."

1. Boil sugar and water to make syrup

2. Add fruit and syrup to a jar

3. Seal and store for later

And one of those laters was...

APPLE PIE!

The Origin of Apple Pie

But how did we get the pie part of apple pie? To look at the origins of apple pie, we have to go back in time again.

The first known apple pie recipe appeared in a cookbook from 1390. Here's part of that pie recipe:

Tak gode Applys and wan they are wel ybrayed coloard wyth Safron wel and do yt in a cofyn and do it forth to bake well.

That's not the English we use today. And they weren't the pies we know today, either. The crusts were called "cofyns."

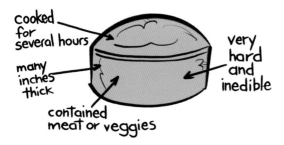

cooked for several hours

many inches thick

very hard and inedible

contained meat or veggies

They were only containers to hold the contents of the pie. They also helped prevent spoilage and made them portable. Cofyns were an early lunchbox!

But everyone has a sweet tooth, and as you already know, by the 1600s sugar was available, though still a luxury. Cooks began to add it to pies and to make pie crusts both sweet and edible.

That's too much!

Keep going!

Pretty soon everyone in Europe was enjoying pies no matter what they were doing.

The American Apple Pie Craze

The British colonists couldn't imagine life without apple pie, and brought them on the journey, along with the original apple trees that failed to grow, and the seeds that eventually did.

Americans loved apple pie (and all pies, really) so much that they ate them for every meal, including breakfast. They didn't just eat pie after dinner. They ate it **for** dinner!

Apple pies were a favorite because they were cheap and easy to prepare with ingredients that most people had in their homes.

And if they were away from home, apple pie was what they craved. During the Civil War soldiers raided farms for apples and flour to make pies.

But how did apple pie become so American? So much so that we say "as American as apple pie?"

Apple pie first became a symbol of America in a 1902 article in the *New York Times* that called apple pie "heroic" and "the American symbol of prosperity." The authors also said,

No pie-eating people can be permanently vanquished.

Soldiers in World War II had a popular slogan:

We are fighting for "mom and apple pie."

Pie was a reminder of home, and what they were fighting for.

Apple pie became a common dessert for American holidays, like the Fourth of July and Thanksgiving. This cemented apple pie's reputation as a food that Americans love.

Apple pie is a lot like America itself. The ingredients came from elsewhere, like the early colonists. However, once apples got here, they developed their own identity, just like the American people.

The Final Course

We've come to the end of our food journey together. If we weren't hungry before, we might be now! But there are probably some foods you like that aren't covered in this book.

There might also be some foods from your family's culture that you serve all the time. Why not learn about your family's food history? Does your family have any foods that have been passed down for generations? Or if your family is from another country, are there food traditions that they brought with them?

So if you have a favorite food, why not find out more about it? You might find some facts that will blow your mind! If I've made you hungry to learn more, read on to find out how to do that.

STILL HUNGRY?

Here's some more to chew on!

How to
be a
food historian

How to
make food
comics

Further
reading

Delicious
recipes

...and more!

HOW TO BE A FOOD HISTORIAN!

I'm sure there's a food you love that this book didn't cover. Are you curious about it? Become a food historian! Here's how.

First, choose a food you like that you are curious about.

Next, go to the internet and search for information. Type [your food] history in the search bar. Don't just use the first source you find! Check out some of the others too.

Books are good sources, too!

Are you curious about how old your food is? Try to find the first recorded evidence of your food being eaten. Who ate it, where was it, and how long ago? It might have been a lot different than it is today!

Maybe you want to know about your food's superheroes. Search for the people who made your food popular, or changed the way it was prepared.

Look for amazing inventions: the advances in technology that helped your food out in a big way.

Look for how-tos. Is there a specific recipe or technique that you have to learn to be able to call yourself an expert on your food?

Pretzel twisting!

Also look for how your food is eaten in different parts of the world.

If you can't find any of those things, don't worry! You can just look for facts that your friends don't know.

The **Laugenbrötchen** is from Germany!

The phrase **"tie the knot"** might come from a custom of giving **pretzels** to couples **getting married**.

Congratulations! You have now earned the title of food historian. Be sure to share your knowledge with the world! (Or at least your family).

FOOD HIST-ORIAN

We are so proud of you! (And hungry!)

How To Create a FOOD COMIC! (or any comic, really)

Step 1:

Plan your script. Do this panel by panel. Don't use too many words! Save room for artwork.

Panel 1: "Noodle making developed during the Han dynasty."

Panel 2: "The job of the t'ang guan was to provide the emperor with noodles."

Step 2:

Once you have your script done, plan out your images.

I'll draw the t'ang guan bringing an enormous bowl of noodles to the emperor.

Step 3:

Now it's time to create! All you need is paper and something to draw with.

You can use anything to create comics. Experiment!

Step 4:

Divide your paper into three rows. Divide the rows into panels. Six is a good number, but you can use as many as you want.

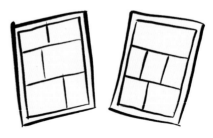

Step 5:

Add words before you draw to make sure you have enough room for the text. If you don't, divide your text into two panels, or take out some of the words.

Not enough room for drawings.

Step 6:

Use the internet for reference photos if you don't know what certain people look like, or what people wore.

Emperor Huan

Step 7:

Don't forget to add backgrounds to your comic. You can do research on the internet or in books to see what buildings looked like during the time period.

Step 8:

Color your work if you want to. Markers tend to bleed. Use crayons or colored pencils instead.

Step 9:

You did it! Share your finished comic with your friends, family, and teachers. Hopefully they will learn something new!

How to Draw People

 Stick figures are boring! You can do better.

 draw a circle for the head

a rectangle for the body

add arms & legs

Play around with shapes. Make your people different from each other.

Kid bodies have the same head size, but smaller body.

BETTER FACES

 Add a nose and eyebrows. (and ears too!)

EXPRESSIONS

ADD HAIR!

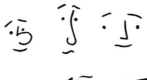

 Have fun with the size and placement of facial features.

HANDS

 FIST

OPEN

 POINTING

 SPREAD (three fingers are plenty)

SAMPLE GESTURES

A sketchbook is a great place to practice and keep good ideas.  SKETCH Book

How To Make A Delicious Meal

Here are instructions to make a meal with some of the foods discussed in this book. You'll want to start with pickles, because you need to make those in advance.

quick and easy pickles

vinegar
water
mason jar
sugar
salt
cucumbers

WHAT YOU NEED

- 2–3 cucumbers
- 1/2 cup of vinegar (any kind)
- 1 cup water
- 1 tablespoon sugar
- 2 teaspoons salt
- A mason jar and a large measuring cup.

DIRECTIONS:

Cutting cucumbers
cut lengthwise

1. Ask an adult for help.

2. Slice the cucumbers into quarters lengthwise, then slice them across so that they will fit in the mason jar. Put in as many slices as you can.

then again

3. In the measuring cup mix the vinegar, water, salt and sugar until the salt and sugar dissolve.

cut across
to fit into jar

4. Pour the liquid over the cucumbers to cover them completely. If the liquid doesn't go all the way to the top, add more water.

5. Screw on the lid to the mason jar and shake. (Not too hard!)

6. Soak the cucumbers overnight in the refrigerator before serving.

Other things you can add: dill, onion, garlic, other vegetables like hot peppers. There are plenty of pickle recipes out there for you to try as your pickle mastery increases!

California club sandwich

WHAT YOU NEED

- 2 slices bread
- sliced turkey breast
- 4 slices of cooked bacon
- 1 avocado
- 1 medium tomato
- lettuce
- mayonnaise

bread
lettuce
tomato
avocado
bacon
turkey
mayo
bread

DIRECTIONS:

1. Get an adult to help you, especially with the slicing.

2. Toast your bread. Or, don't! It's up to you.

3. Thinly slice the avocados and tomatoes.

4. Assemble as shown.

Finally, you can finish off your meal with a delicious  milkshake!

WHAT YOU NEED

- 2 scoops vanilla ice cream
- 1 teaspoon sugar
- 2 cups milk
- chocolate sauce
- a blender

blender

milk

ice cream

sugar

chocolate syrup

DIRECTIONS:

1. Get an adult to help you with the tricky stuff.

2. Add all of the ingredients to the blender and mix thoroughly.

3. If your milkshake seems too thick, add more milk. If it seems too runny, add more ice cream. Don't add too much! A little goes a long way.

4. Add your milkshake to a large glass. Grab a straw, or a spoon if you made it too thick to drink.

You can also add whipped cream on top, and maybe a cherry.

Enjoy right away! Especially on hot days.

Further Reading

Books on Food History

Eamer, Claire. *The World in Your Lunchbox: The Wacky History and Weird Science of Everyday Foods.*
Toronto: Annick Press, 2012.

Gates, Stefan. *Science You Can Eat: 20 Activities that Put Food Under the Microscope.* New York, NY:
DK Children, 2019.

Reilly, Kathleen M. *Food: 25 Amazing Projects Investigate the History and Science of What We Eat (Build It Yourself).*
Norwich, VT: Nomad Press, 2010.

Steel, Tanya. *Food Fight: A Mouthwatering History of Who Ate What and Why Through the Ages.*
Washington, DC: National Geographic Kids, 2018.

Zachman, Kim. *There's No Ham in Hamburgers: Facts and Folklore About Our Favorite Foods.*
Philadelphia: Running Press Kids, 2021.

Cookbooks

America's Test Kitchen Kids. *The Complete Baking Book for Young Chefs: 100+ Sweet and Savory Recipes that You'll
Love to Bake, Share and Eat!.* Naperville, IL: Sourcebooks eXplore, 2019.

Food Network Magazine, editor. *The Big, Fun Kids Baking Book: 100+ Recipes for Young Bakers.*
New York: Hearst Home Kids, 2021.

Websites

The Food Timeline: foodtimeline.org

History Channel Food Stories: history.com/tag/food/

History Today Food and Drink Articles: historytoday.com/themes/food-drink/

National Geographic Food Resources: education.nationalgeographic.org/resource/food/

Smithsonian Magazine Food Stories: smithsonianmag.com/category/food/

What's Cooking American Food History: whatscookingamerica.net/history/historyindex.htm

Books for Teachers and Parents

Pollan, Michael. *The Omnivore's Dilemma: A Natural History of Four Meals.* New York: Penguin, 2007.

Reese, Jennifer. *Make the Bread, Buy the Butter: What You Should and Shouldn't Cook from Scratch.*
New York: Atria Books, 2011.

Siegel, Matt. *The Secret History of Food: Strange but True Stories About the Origins of Everything We Eat.*
New York: Ecco, 2021.

Wilson, Bee. *Consider the Fork: A History of How We Cook and Eat.* New York: Basic Books, 2010.

Index

Acknowledgments

There are several people who helped me bring this book from a recipe to a final course.

First, I want to thank my editor Harold Underdown for his guidance, wisdom, and encouragement along the way. He understood the kind of book I wanted to create and helped me get there.

I also owe a huge thank you to my agent, Janna Morishima, who believed I could create something wonderful for kids. She helped steer me in the right direction and was a great cheerleader and mentor.

Juliana, Barbara, Symon, and everyone else at Kane Press.

I would also like to thank Renee Harleston of *Writing Diversely* for her sensitivity read, and a respected food historian who asked not to be credited for feedback on history.

This book would never have happened if it weren't for my friend Caitlin Mitchell. A chance discussion about taking on new challenges led me to attempt my first graphic novel. Also, Mary Montero was an early advocate for doing something different with my passion for comics and helped me come up with ideas for a younger audience.

I have the best critique group in the world. Sarah Giles, Cesar Lador, Lana Le, and Ken Rolston gave me a host of good ideas and some much needed guidance.

Jenny Robb, Anne Drozd, and Cailtin McGurk at the Billy Ireland Cartoon Museum for treating me like an actual comics creator and providing inspiration along the way.

To my parents: you have supported me in everything I do whether it be buying endless reams of paper and art supplies when I was a kid or hanging my art at your house or office. I love you both and you got me where I am today.

To my kids Jack and Lily: you are the reason I do everything, including this book. You make my life fuller each day. I hope you are proud of what I did.

To my wife Julie for putting up with my idiosyncrasies, like drawing comics. I'm not sure you knew that was going to be part of the deal, but I thank you for giving me the time to work on this and being an occasional reader. I love you and your support means the world to me.

And finally to Bingley and Pemberley, our dogs, for coming into the office occasionally for pats on the head.

About the Author

David grew up in Columbus, Ohio, surrounded by stacks of *MAD Magazines*, Calvin and Hobbes collections, and Walt Disney comics. He spent most of his free time learning about sable hair brushes, non-repro blue pencils, and Bristol board so he could pursue a career drawing a comic strip.

However, he went to Ohio State University instead to pursue a degree in education. But he never gave up on the dream! He drew a daily strip in *The Lantern* (Ohio State University's school newspaper) for most of his college years. After receiving a teaching degree and spending a few years in the classroom, the itch to create comics resurfaced. He headed back to the drawing board (literally) to create educational comics, selling them on the Teachers Pay Teachers marketplace. Educators from around the world have enthusiastically embraced his comics as an effective way to approach difficult language arts concepts, especially to reluctant readers and English language learners.

When he's not drawing comics, David likes to do yoga, play guitar, and read.

Pizza, Pickles, and Apple Pie is his first graphic novel.